Penguin English
Introducing Classroom Interaction

Amy B. M. Tsui is Senior Lecturer of the Department of Curriculum Studies and Director of The Teachers of English Language Education Centre (TELEC) at the University of Hong Kong. She has taught at secondary and tertiary levels in Hong Kong and Singapore. At present, she is a teacher educator specializing in language teacher education. She has published in the following areas: classroom interaction, discourse analysis, conversational analysis, speech act theory and teacher education.

Ronald Carter is Professor of Modern English Language in the Department of English Studies at the University of Nottingham. He is the author of many books on applied linguistics and was the National Co-ordinator for the LINC (Language in the National Curriculum) project from 1989 to 1992.

David Nunan is Professor of Applied Linguistics and Director of the English Centre at the University of Hong Kong. He has worked as a TESOL teacher, teacher educator, curriculum designer, and materials writer and consultant in Britain and overseas and is the author of many books on applied linguistics and ELT.

Other Titles in the Series

Introducing

CLASSROOM INTERACTION

Amy B. M. Tsui

Series Editors:
Ronald Carter and David Nunan

PENGUIN
ENGLISH

PENGUIN ENGLISH

Published by the Penguin Group
Penguin Books Ltd, 27 Wrights Lane, London W8 5TZ, England
Penguin Books USA Inc., 375 Hudson Street, New York, New York 10014, USA
Penguin Books Australia Ltd, Ringwood, Victoria, Australia
Penguin Books Canada Ltd, 10 Alcorn Avenue, Toronto, Ontario, Canada M4V 3B2
Penguin Books (NZ) Ltd, 182–190 Wairau Road, Auckland 10, New Zealand

Penguin Books Ltd, Registered Offices: Harmondsworth, Middlesex, England

First published 1995
10 9 8 7 6 5 4 3 2 1

Typeset by Datix International Limited, Bungay, Suffolk
Set in Lasercomp Times Roman
Printed in England by Clays Ltd, St Ives plc

For Chi-kin

The insights provided by work in applied linguistics can be of genuine support to all teachers facing the many complex demands of language learning and teaching. The Penguin English *Introducing Applied Linguistics* series aims to provide short, clear and accessible guides to key topics – helping teachers to keep abreast of this rapidly developing field by explaining recent research and its relevance to common problems and concerns. The books are designed for practical use: they focus on recognizable classroom contexts, suggest problem-solving approaches, and include activities and questions for further study.

Introducing Applied Linguistics presumes an increasing convergence of interest among all English language teachers, and it aims to be relevant both to teachers of English as a second or foreign language and to teachers of English as a mother tongue. As the relationship between linguistics and language teaching continues to develop, so the need grows for books which introduce the field. This series has been developed to meet that need.

The words that appear in **bold** type are
explained in the glossary.

Acknowledgements

I am deeply grateful to my students, most of whom are practising teachers, who are a constant source of inspiration. I thank them for allowing me to record their lessons and, in some cases, to use their classroom data. Their reactions to my lectures, on which this book is based, and their interpretations of the classroom data that I included in this book have helped me to gain a deeper understanding of the complexities of classroom processes. I am also deeply grateful to Ron Carter for encouraging me to write for this series and to David Nunan for his insightful comments on the first draft of the manuscript. To Chi-kin, my husband, I owe the greatest debt. I thank him for being most understanding and supportive.

Contents

Contents

Introduction

The aim of this book is to raise language teachers' awareness of the complexities of classroom language teaching and learning. It is intended to help teachers develop sensitivity towards the language they use in the classroom, the interaction generated, and the effects on student participation and learning, and it introduces various approaches to making systematic observations of the classroom. The discussion will be illustrated with language classroom data throughout. Activities are included that require teachers to examine classroom data. At the end of each chapter there are also projects that require teachers to examine their own classrooms, the language they have used and the interaction they have generated.

Chapter 1 is a general introduction to the nature of the classroom. It presents classroom learning as a co-operative effort between the teacher and the students. It points out that how the teacher and the students interact, and how students interact amongst themselves, affect the opportunities for language learning. The main purpose of the chapter is to overview aspects of classroom interaction that are relevant to language learning.

Chapter 2 focuses on the language used by the teacher. It starts with teachers' questions, which take up the greatest percentage of teacher talk in most language classrooms. The issue of what makes a question more or less difficult will be addressed. The classification of questions and their effects on student response will also be discussed. Explanation – an important aspect of teacher talk that is largely neglected in classroom interaction studies – is also dealt with in detail. Finally, the role of feedback in language learning is examined. Teachers' perception and treatment of errors are investigated.

Chapter 3 examines the concept of comprehensible input and how it can be achieved by modifying the input as well as the interaction between the teacher and the students. It points out the importance of student involvement in making the input comprehensible and in the negotiation of meaning. The turn-taking system in the classroom is also discussed in the light of how teachers' turn allocation affects student learning and how students' turn-taking behaviours are affected by their cultural background.

Chapter 4 focuses on student response and participation. The problem of getting student response in language classrooms is discussed in the light of research done on language learning anxiety. The value of small group talk is discussed in terms of how it both helps students to overcome language learning anxiety and encourages them to engage in meaningful communication.

Chapter 5 discusses two different approaches to classroom observation: systematic and ethnographic. It briefly outlines the limitations of systematic observation and suggests that it should be used complementarily with the ethnographic approach.

In extracts from classroom conversation, a square bracket – [– indicates overlapping speech, and an equals sign – = – indicates an utterance that is continuous but is separated because of the transcription format.

1 Classroom interaction and language learning

1.1 The nature of the classroom

The classroom can be defined as a place where more than two people gather together for the purpose of learning, with one having the role of teacher. The teacher has certain perceptions about his or her role in the classroom. Consider the following excerpt taken from an ESL teacher's journal:

I felt . . . that I spoke too much in the classroom, and that my students did not participate enough. I am now more aware of <u>why</u> this was so: subconsciously, I felt that as I am the teacher, I should dominate the lesson; in fact I didn't trust the students' ability to think for themselves, they must have sensed this and such an atmosphere can only devalue the whole classroom learning experience.

This particular teacher's perception of his role as the key player resulted in him dominating the classroom talk. Teachers also have certain expectations about how business should be conducted in the classroom. For example, when students answer questions, they should put up their hands; answers that are provided without observing such classroom protocol will not be accepted even if they are appropriate. The teacher also has certain ideas about how the lesson should proceed, what kinds of questions to ask, what kinds of activities they want students to do, and what they expect students to get out of this lesson. Lessons are judged as good or bad on the basis of whether they turn out the way they were planned and whether the expected outcome is achieved.

However, all teachers know there is often a gap between what

1

they want to achieve and what actually happens, because there are many factors that affect classroom interaction.

ACTIVITY

The following is an excerpt from a Primary Four ESL reading comprehension lesson. When you come to the questions, answer them first; try to resist the temptation to read the following text.

1a
(The teacher has just finished giving instructions to pupils about their grammar homework and answering pupils' questions about homework.)

S: *Do we need to draw a picture?*
T: *Draw what picture?*
S: *The*
 [
T: *No, you don't have to draw the pictures, just write just write the sentences. All right, now will you take out your green book four.*

At this point, what do you think the teacher's planned sequence is? After you have answered this question, continue to read the data to see if the lesson progresses as planned.

S: *Mrs Kent, do we need to write number one on the book?*
T: *No, you don't have to write number one, otherwise it would be twelve pairs of sentences, wouldn't it? Eleven pairs.*
S: *Do we get the green book four?*
T: *Green book four, yes. You know it's reading lesson, why don't you get it out ready? All right, now, green book four. Last week, we were reading Kee Knock Stan. What is Kee Knock Stan? Janice.*
Ja: *I cannot understand.*
T: *Yes. And what language is it supposed to be? Julia.*
Ju: *Lalloon language.*

2

T: Right. And where is Lalloon Land supposed to be?

Ss: (Silence).

T: Do you think there is a real country called Lalloon Land?

Ss: No.

T: No. But in the story, what does it say about Lalloon Land?

Ss: (Silence)

T: Have you been to Lalloon Land?

Ss: (shake heads)

S: (raises hand)

T: Michele?

What do you think Michele is going to say? After you have answered this question, continue to read the data and see how the progress of the lesson is affected by what Michele says.

S: Can we give in our grammar on um Wednesday?

T: Can you give in your grammar on Wednesday? You have a lot of homework for tomorrow?

Ss: Yes, yes.

S: We have our last exercise.

T: You have to do –

S: Our last exercise.

T: Oh that's because you have been lazy and didn't do your work properly. That's why you have extra work to do. Right?

Ss: No.

T: So I'm sorry, you have to do it, otherwise I won't be able to finish marking your books to give you back before the holidays.

Now that the teacher has dealt with the request for postponing the homework deadline, what do you think she would want to do? After answering this question, see what actually happened in the following.

(Several students went up to the teacher to ask questions about the homework book that was given back to them at the beginning of the lesson.)

3

T: *Have a quick look at your grammar books because a few of you*
   don't seem to know what's wrong with your work.
(Teacher carries on with her conversation with students who went
up to her.)
S: (inaudible)
T: *I'm using two marks.*
S: *Only six.*
T: *Only six. Then that means twelve marks and you've got twenty-*
   nine. So that means you've been missing not quite six.
S: (nods head)
(Author's data)

As we can see from the above piece of data, the lesson did not
proceed according to the teacher's plan. Obviously, the teacher and
the pupils had different concerns: the teacher was keen to get on
with the lesson and start teaching the reading passage; the pupils,
however, were worried about getting the instructions for homework right, not having enough time to finish their homework, and
not understanding the assessment of their homework. It was not
until the teacher had allayed their anxieties that she was able to
carry on the lesson as planned.

Allwright and Bailey (1991: 25) used the term 'derailment' to
describe lessons which, as it were, ran off the tracks, that is, did not
go according to the planned sequence. Consider the following
incident, which is reported by an ESL teacher in his weekly
journal. He reported how a student contribution changed the
direction of a writing lesson.

1b

Monday, 18 November
   Review common errors from the summary. I decided to try a new
strategy: rather than ask students to call out their suggested correc-
tions, I had them come up to the board and correct them in coloured
chalk. (I feel students should write on the board more often than they
do . . . also, there is a much greater loss of face for them if they do

make a mistake when they are physically standing in front of their classmates.)

Naturally, no one volunteered to come up but those called on came up willingly enough. That is, until Jackson confidently called out the correct version to his sentence thus obviating the need for him to move from his seat. From then on everyone else preferred to answer orally rather than write. The pace was a bit brisker today compared with last week's session, but still not really satisfactory.

Overall the atmosphere was much warmer, with more laughter and smiles in evidence.

(Author's data)

We can see from the teacher's journal that the decision of the student, Jackson, not to follow the teacher's instruction in fact had a positive effect on the pace and the atmosphere of the lesson. If the teacher had not allowed the lesson to 'derail', it might not have been as lively as it was. In other words, teachers' willingness to pick up cues from students and make on-the-spot decisions to modify their plans is an important element in classroom interaction.

Gaies (1980) describes the classroom as the 'crucible' in which elements interact. These elements, as we have seen from the above examples, are the teacher and the students. And as Allwright and Bailey point out, apart from teacher expectations, students also 'bring with them their whole experience of learning and of life in classrooms, along with their own reasons for being there, and their own particular needs that they hope to see satisfied' (1991: 18). These elements constantly interact with each other, and it is the chemistry among these elements that determines the progress of the lesson, the kind of learning opportunities that are made available and finally the learning that takes place.

ACTIVITY

The following is an extract from the journal of a teacher who tried to change his style of teaching from teacher-centred to more learner-centred. He tried to attend more to cues from students instead of sticking to his own planned procedures. What happened to his attempt to change his teaching style? How did he deal with the students' reactions?

1c

I have since made a conscious effort to modify my behaviour: I digress much more in pursuit of the students' line of thought and I attempt to hand over the floor to others whenever possible; in short, I am endeavouring to remove the focus from myself and devolve the responsibility for learning on the students themselves ... I detect some resistance from a number of students as this change in my behaviour is violating their expectations of what I should be doing ... As a compromise, I am providing them with hand-outs (particularly in English Literature), despite laying myself open to the charge of 'spoon-feeding'.
(Author's data)

We can see from the teacher's journal that the students' expectations of the teacher are as important as the teacher's expectations in determining the way a lesson proceeds. Students who expect the teacher to stick very closely to the textbook or the teaching material may find it disconcerting when he or she digresses into topics that, in their view, are tenuously related to the subject-matter of the lesson. Students who see the teacher as the giving end of knowledge and themselves as the passive receiving end may not welcome the opportunity to take responsibility for their learning. Such expectations cannot be ignored since they impinge on the classroom atmosphere, which affects classroom interaction and learning. As Allwright and Bailey (1991: 18–19) point out, 'the success of the interaction between the elements in the classroom cannot be taken for granted and cannot be guaranteed just by exhaustive planning.' This is because classroom interaction – in fact interaction of any kind – is a co-operative effort among participants. Each participant has as much to contribute as every other participant in determining the direction and outcome of the interaction. As Allwright and

Bailey (1991: 18–19) further point out, 'interaction, in class or anywhere, has to be managed, as it goes along, no matter how much has gone into it beforehand ... it has to be managed by everyone taking part, not just by the teacher, because interaction is obviously not something you just do <u>to</u> people, but something people do <u>together</u>, collectively.'

1.2 Classroom interaction and learning

Studies in first-language classrooms, both primary and secondary, have shown that the language used by the teacher affects the language produced by the learners, the interaction generated and hence the kind of learning that takes place.

Wells (1986), in a study that compares children's language at home and at school, found that children in school speak with adults much less that at home, get fewer speaking turns and ask fewer questions. The meanings that they express are of a smaller range and the sentences they use are syntactically much simpler. The reason is that teachers do most of the talking in the classroom, determine the topic of talk, and initiate most of the questions and requests. As a result, students are reduced to a very passive role of answering questions and carrying out the teacher's instructions. Wells also found that, while parents often incorporate meanings offered in children's utterances, teachers tend to develop meanings that they themselves have introduced into the conversation, and expect students to follow the teacher's line of thinking rather than the other way round.

ACTIVITY

The following is a conversation that occurred in a preschool play group. Do you notice any difference in Lee's language as the conversation progresses? If there is, what do you think has caused it?

7

1d

(Lee is at school. He has found a horse chestnut and brings it to his teacher to show her.)

Lee: *I want to show you! Isn't it big?*

Teacher: *It is big, isn't it? What is it?*

Lee: *A conker.*

Teacher: *Yes.*

Lee: *Then that'll need opening up.*

Teacher: *It needs opening up. What does it need opening up for?*

Lee: *'Cos the seed's inside.*

Teacher: *Yes, very good. What will the seed grow into?*

Lee: *A conker.*

Teacher: *No, it won't grow into a conker. It'll grow into a sort of tree, won't it? Can you remember the –*

Lee: *Horse chestnut.*

Teacher: *Horse chestnut – good. Put your conker on the nature table then.*

(Wood *et al.* 1980, cited in Wells, 1986: 88)

In this piece of data, as Wells points out, the child Lee starts off with something that he is interested in and wants to share with the teacher. The teacher, with all her good intentions, tries to help the child extend his knowledge by relating the conker to the tree that it came from and will later grow into. However, Wells observes, by doing so the teacher is imposing her agenda on the child instead of trying to find out what the child wanted to share with her and the topic he is interested in. As we can see from the data, as soon as the teacher asks the question '*What does it need opening up for?*', the nature of the interaction changes from the child sharing his observations with the teacher to a didactic question–answer sequence where the child provides shorter and shorter answers to the teacher's questions.

ACTIVITY

Consider the following piece of classroom conversation, which is an excerpt from a Primary One social studies lesson in a Hong Kong school. Look at how the students respond to the teacher's explanation and their interaction among themselves. What do you think they are trying to do? Look at the teacher's response to the students' contributions. What do you think she is trying to do?

1e

(The teacher is telling pupils about traffic-lights and what the various signals mean.)

T: Yes. It (that is, when the green light flickers) *tells us that pedestrians should not cross the road. They should stay on the pavement and not cross the road because the light is about to change. It tells the pedestrians to stop crossing the road.*

S: *Teacher, I have something to tell you.*

T: *Yes?*

S: *There are three safe ways of crossing the road. The first one is the overhead bridge, and the subway and the zebra crossing. But if cars have not stopped completely, don't ever start crossing the road.*

T: *That's right, that's right.*

S: *You have to let the driver go first.*

T: *Thank you. Chi Chun. Good boy. Sit down. We'll talk about this later. Clever boy.*

S: (raises hand)

T: *Yes, King Yin.*

S: *Some of them have got circles. Once the pedestrians step on to the road, the cars will stop.*

T: *Yes. Then, children –*

S: (raises hand)

T: *Yes, Ling Fung.*

S: *Some roads have traffic-lights where there is a button which says 'Wait'. And when the green light comes on, the 'Wait' sign goes off.*

T: *That's right. OK. So, children, you have to pay special attention. These lights* (s

> *for cars, they are for drivers. But these lights* (showing the children another traffic-light model) *are for pedestrians. You have to pay special attention. Wait for the green light to come on before you cross the road.*

(Author's data; translated from Chinese)

We can see from the enthusiastic contributions of the pupils that they are bringing in their own experience and knowledge of the world to relate to what the teacher is telling them. Ironically, the pupils' knowledge of road safety is far more sophisticated than what the teacher planned to teach – what the three colours of the traffic-lights mean. The teacher could have used the pupils' contributions as a springboard for further discussion, thus helping them to construct knowledge on the basis of what they know already and what they have observed. However, as we can see from the teacher's utterance at the end of the above excerpt, she is keen to get back to her agenda for this lesson. The teacher's summary of what she set out to teach pales against the pupils' contributions.

ACTIVITY

The following is a conversation in which the child Elizabeth, four years old, is watching her mother shovel wood ash from the grate into a bucket. Compare it with texts 1d and 1e above and discuss whether there is any difference in the nature of the interaction and the language of the mother and child.

1f

Elizabeth: *What are you doing that for?*
Mother: *I'm gathering it up and putting it outside so that Daddy can put it on the garden.*
Elizabeth: *Why does he have to put it on the garden?*
Mother: *To make the compost right.*
Elizabeth: *Does that make the grass grow?*
Mother: *Yes.*
Elizabeth: *Why does it?*

Mother: *You know how I tell you that you need to eat different things like eggs and cabbage and rice pudding to make you grow into a big girl.*

Elizabeth: *Yes.*

Mother: *Well, plants need different foods too. And ash is one of the things that's good for them.*

(Wells 1986: 59)

One very obvious difference in the nature of the interaction between this piece of parent–child conversation and the teacher–pupil conversation in text **1d** is that the questions are all initiated by the child rather than by the adult. The child, as Wells points out, is trying to make sense of the world by asking questions, and to pose further questions on the basis of the answers. The mother, on the other hand, tries to help the child to understand how wood ash makes grass grow by making use of her existing knowledge. The child, and not the adult, is in control of the topic.

From the examples given above we can see that the language used affects the nature of the interaction, which in turn affects the opportunities for learning that are made available. The study of classroom language and interaction is therefore central to the study of classroom learning. As van Lier (1988: 77–78) points out, 'If the keys to learning are exposure to input and meaningful interaction with other speakers, we must find out what input and interaction the classroom can provide . . . We must study in detail the use of language in the classroom in order to see if and how learning comes about through the different ways of interacting in the classroom.'

1.3   Classroom interaction and language learning

In 1.2 we discussed the importance of classroom language and interaction in first-language classrooms of content subjects. In the language classroom, be it first, second or foreign language, classroom language and interaction are even more important because language is at once the subject of study as well as the medium for learning. When students listen to the teacher's instructions and explanations, when they express their views, answer questions and carry out tasks and activities, they are not only learning about the language but also putting the language that they are learning to use. In situations where the target language is seldom used outside the classroom and the students' exposure to the target language is therefore mainly in the classroom, the kind of input and interaction that is made available is particularly important.

Krashen (1977) makes a distinction between conscious learning and naturalistic acquisition in second-language learning. He argues that classroom instructions directed at the conscious learning of rules is of limited value in terms of helping learners acquire the target language. However, Long (1983a) observes that the relative success of advanced learners in instructional settings over learners who acquire the language naturally means that instruction has an important role to play in language acquisition. Although it is unclear exactly in what way instruction contributes to the learner's language development, it is clear that instruction does make a difference. This could well be due to the fact that in ESL or EFL classrooms both conscious and unconscious learning of the target language takes place. When the teacher is teaching an item explicitly and getting students to practise it, then conscious learning is going on; but when the teacher relates anecdotes or students relate their own experiences and express their ideas, unconscious acquisition is occurring.

1.4 Aspects of classroom interaction

In this section we shall outline the aspects of classroom interaction that will be of relevance to language learning. Each aspect will then be elaborated in subsequent chapters.

ACTIVITY

Look at the following conversation taken from an S2 (Grade 8) ESL classroom. Would you say that it is fairly typical of classroom exchanges? What is the pattern of interaction? Would you say that it is a dominant interaction pattern in classrooms?

1g

T: *Christmas is coming. What are you going to do?* (pause) *Christmas is coming. Do you like Christmas?*

Ss: *Yes . . . No.*

T: *So what are you going to do?*

S: *I'll write –*

T: *Yes, Alex, can you tell me?*

S: *I'll write some Christmas cards.*

T: *You'll write some Christmas cards. To who? Girlfriends?*

Ss: (laughs)

T: *To your friends, right . . .*

(Author's data)

The dominant pattern of interaction is that of teacher question, student response and teacher feedback, which is commonly found in all classrooms and is typical of classroom exchanges. As we can see, teacher talk not only takes up the largest portion of talk but also determines the topic of talk and who talks. It is therefore a very important component of classroom interaction.

1.4.1 Teacher questions

ACTIVITY

Consider text **1g** again. What is teacher talk largely made up of? What aspects of the teacher's talk would be of relevance to students' production of the target language?

In text **1g** teacher questions take up a very high percentage of the teacher's talk. Educational studies on classroom language have examined the cognitive demands of teacher questions and their effects on students' learning. Studies on ESL classrooms, however, have focused on the effect of teacher questions on learners' production of the target language and on the types of learner response.

In text **1g** the teacher introduces the topic of Christmas and directs a question at the whole class. She modifies her question when no response is forthcoming. After the students have answered the modified question as a group, the teacher then puts the previous question again to the students. This time a student, Alex, attempts to answer the teacher's question. The modification of questions to make them comprehensible to students and to elicit response is another important area of classroom interaction. We can see in text **1g** that, in order to elicit responses from students, the teacher modified her question from a wh-question (what? why? where? etc.) to a yes–no question to minimize the linguistic demand made on the students. In chapter 2 we shall discuss the various types of teacher questions, what functions they serve and how teachers modify their questions to help learners to understand and participate in the discourse.

1.4.2 Teacher feedback and error treatment

Teacher feedback on responses given by students is another very important element in classroom interaction. Students need to know whether they have correctly understood the teacher and have provided the appropriate answer. They are likely to feel frustrated if the teacher keeps withholding feedback.

ACTIVITY

Examine the following conversation from an S2 ESL lesson. Look at the way the teacher responds to the students' answers. What is the teacher trying to do?

1h

(The teacher has asked the students to conduct an interview. She is going over the questions that they have asked in the interview. She points at the words 'teaching experience' on the blackboard and asks students what question they have asked in relation to that.)

S: *How many years do you teaching?*

T: *How many years do you – ?* (points at the same student)

S: *Teaching.*

T: *Teach, teaching in this school? Who can help? It's not very right, I'm afraid. It's not very, it's not very very right. It should be? Yes? Monitor, you look very smart today.*

Ss: (laugh)

Monitor: *How long have you been teaching in this school?*

T: (writes on the blackboard) *How long have you been teaching in this school . . .*

(Wu 1991: TA8)

The question that the student asks in relation to teaching experience is appropriate in terms of content but inaccurate in terms of form. The teacher, instead of explicitly rejecting the answer, tries to get the student to produce the question again. The student, apparently interpreting the teacher's utterance not as a request to reformulate the question but as a request to repeat the last part of the question, simply adds the word *teaching* to the teacher's previous utterance. The teacher then makes her intention clear by asking if other students could help, followed by an explicit statement that the answer is not quite right. Up to this point she has not specified what is not quite right about the question. It is not until the monitor produces the question in the correct grammatical form that she accepts the answer by repeating the question and putting it on the board.

This sequence of interaction is commonly found in language classrooms. Teachers tend to require students to produce the target language correctly both in content and form. What is interesting in the above piece of data is the way the teacher provides feedback to the students and the students' interpretation of the feedback.

In the language classroom, what the teacher considers as appropriate contributions and errors is very important, not only in terms of getting students to produce the target language and to engage in meaningful communication, but also in terms of their understanding of how the language works. In chapter 2 we shall look at what teachers consider as errors, how they deal with them and what kind of feedback they provide.

1.4.3 Teacher explanation

Another component that takes up a significant portion of teacher talk is explanation. There are different ways of defining explanation. Some define it very generally as providing information or communicating content, others make a distinction between explanation of procedures and explanation of concepts, vocabulary and grammatical rules. How teachers deal with explanation is very important. Inappropriate explanation or over-explanation hinder rather than help students to comprehend.

ACTIVITY

In the following text, which is a continuation of text **1h** above, the teacher is trying to explain the word 'experience'. What strategy is the teacher using, and is it effective?

1i

T: . . . Er, you all know this word teaching, to teach. All right?
Teaching. Experience, that is what? (looks around the class)
How much you know about something and what er how long you
have done something – er – for example you have done a certain
thing for a long time. You know a lot about it, so you are

experienced. You know the word experienced, right? (points to the blackboard) *So how long have you been teaching in this school? . . .*

(Wu 1991: TA8)

The teacher is trying to explain the word *experience* by relating it to a word that students know already, *experienced*. This is a commonly used strategy in vocabulary explanation. There are other kinds of strategies that teachers use, such as examples, gestures, anecdotes and so on. In chapter 2 we shall examine strategies used by teachers in both vocabulary and grammar explanation and the characteristics of effective explanation.

1.4.4 Modified input and interaction

Earlier studies of classroom interaction have focused on the features of teachers' speech and the ways in which it is different from their speech outside the classroom. These features are speech rate, syntax, intonation and vocabulary. It is found that, in order to make their speech comprehensible to learners, teachers tend to modify their speech by speaking more slowly, using exaggerated intonation, giving prominence to key words, using simpler syntax and a more basic set of vocabulary. More recent studies have pointed out that simply modifying the input is no guarantee that the input has been made comprehensible to students. On examining conversations between native speakers and non-native speakers, it was found that typically these conversations contain many modification devices such as comprehension checks, requests for repetition and clarification, and confirmation checks. This results in the modification not only of the input but also of the structure of the interaction.

ACTIVITY

Consider the following piece of classroom conversation. What would the interaction have been if the teacher's question was comprehensible to the student from the start? In what way was the interaction structure modified in the process of making the input comprehensible?

1j

T: ... Then er what other advantages do you think you may have, if you were the only child in the family?

S: I'm sorry. I beg your pardon.

T: Er, if you were the only child in your family, then what other advantages you may have? What points, what other good points you may have?

S: It's quieter for my study.

T: Yes? It's quieter for you to study. Yes? Any other?

S: No more.

T: OK, fine.

(Wu 1991: TD7)

The teacher's question is incomprehensible to the student, because he either cannot hear it or cannot catch its meaning. The student therefore requests a repetition of the question from teacher. However, instead of giving an exact repetition, the teacher fronts the conditional clause. This is followed by a paraphrase of *advantages* as *good points* to make it easier for the student to understand. The student then produces a response that is accepted by the teacher. As a result of this attempt by the student to make the input comprehensible, the interaction structure is modified from 'question–answer–feedback' to 'question–request for repetition–repetition followed by a modified question–answer–feedback'.

Modification devices can be used by the teacher or the student in the process of negotiating comprehensible input. While modification devices used by both teachers and students have been taken as indicators of the amount of negotiation work that is going on, hence the amount of comprehensible input made available, it is devices used by students that are the better indicators. This is because, when students are actually involved in making the input comprehensible, it is more likely that the input will be made comprehensible. In chapter 3 we shall examine the ways in which input and interaction are modified in providing and obtaining comprehensible input. It will be argued that student involvement is a very important dimension in the negotiation of comprehensible input.

1.4.5 Turn-allocation and turn-taking behaviours

Whether students are actively involved in classroom interaction is largely determined by the turn-allocation behaviour of the teacher and turn-taking behaviour of the students. To allocate turns to all students is something that all teachers strive to achieve and which they often believe they have achieved. In chapter 3 we will show that this is often not the case.

As for the turn-taking behaviour of students, it is often thought that students either take turns that are solicited by the teacher or initiate turns by asking questions, making requests or volunteering answers. Allwright (1980) found that in fact some shy students take 'private turns' by giving answers or making comments that are for themselves instead of for the rest of the class. In chapter 3 we point out that teachers can look out for these private turns and, if desirable, try to help students make these private turns public. We point out that it is also important to consider cultural factors when looking at the turn-taking behaviour of students.

The emphasis on the involvement of students in classroom interaction seems to imply that there is a causal relationship between turn-taking and language achievement. Seliger (1977) proposes that there are two types of language learners: high-input generators (HIGs) and low-input generators (LIGs). The former participate actively in conversations and consequently generate plenty of input from other people. The latter, by contrast, participate minimally and hence deprive themselves of obtaining input from other people. Seliger maintains that HIGs are more successful language learners than LIGs. However, whether the relationship between input generation and language achievement is a causal one is controversial. In chapter 3 we will also explore this issue in greater detail.

1.4.6 Student talk

Consider the following conversation from an S2 ESL classroom. The teacher has asked a question that is syntactically and lexically simple. However, there is not a single response from the students even after the teacher repeats the question seven times. What do you think is happening?

1k

(In the previous exchange a student answered the teacher by saying 'The boys put up their tent in the middle of the field.')

T: *Who is sitting in the middle of the classroom?*
   Who is sitting in the middle of the classroom?
   Who?
   Who is sitting in the middle of the classroom?
   Who?
   (nominates)
   Who?
S: (silence)
T: *Who is sitting in the middle of the classroom?*
   Who?
S: (silence)
T: *Never mind, sit down.*
   (nominates)
S: *Lau Siu Ling.*
T: *You can say Lau Siu Ling, or you can say nobody, if you like.*
   There is nobody sitting in the middle of the classroom.

(Tsui 1992: 54)

What is happening in the above excerpt is that the teacher is pointing to the middle of the classroom where there is nobody sitting. Her question puzzles the students, including the first one nominated, who, quite understandably, thinks they are supposed to give the name of a particular student; this is why no answer is forthcoming despite the teacher's repetitions. The second student nominated simply takes the risk and names a student who is sitting very near where the teacher is pointing. If the students had told the teacher what the problem was by saying, 'I don't understand what you mean. There is nobody sitting in the middle of the classroom', then there would not have been this breakdown in communication.

The situation in text **1k** is not uncommon in classrooms. Getting students to respond to teacher questions, even just to indicate problems in comprehension or communication, and to participate in class discussion is a problem that many teachers face. A study of three secondary ESL teachers found that about 40 per cent of their questions received no response. Even when the questions were repeated as many as nine times, the teacher still often failed to get a response (White and Lightbown 1984). There are many reasons for questions not being responded to, some having to do with the question itself, as we have already seen, some, however, having to do with the psychological aspects of classroom language learning. In chapter 4 we shall discuss the latter phenomenon in greater detail. We point out that students' reluctance to volunteer answers and to raise questions is often related to anxiety.

An effective way to alleviate this anxiety is to remove the performative and evaluative nature of speaking in class. This can be achieved by group work, where students interact with their peers in a collaborative manner. In terms of language learning, group work provides students with the opportunity to engage in genuine communication, where they produce coherent discourse rather than isolated sentences, hence helping them to acquire discourse competence rather than linguistic competence. In chapter 4 we shall discuss in greater detail the value and features of small group talk.

PROJECT

Take a single lesson and write a lesson plan. The lesson plan should contain the following:
— Aim
— Objectives
— Teaching materials
— Activities
— Procedures
— Learning Outcome

Video-record or audio-record this lesson. View or listen to the recording as many times as you wish. Compare the lesson plan with what went on in the lesson. Ask yourself whether the lesson departed from your lesson plan. If yes, when and why?

SUMMARY

- The classroom is not a place where the teacher just carries out predetermined routines, but rather a place where various elements interact. These elements are the students and the teacher, including their educational and social backgrounds, experience, knowledge and expectations.

- How a lesson progresses and whether it is successful largely depends on the interaction between the students and the teacher. An understanding of the interaction between these elements is, therefore, very important.

- In language classrooms, where the target language is used as a medium of communication, classroom interaction becomes even more important since the target language is at once the subject of learning and the medium of learning.

2 Teacher talk

2.1 Questions

Studies of teachers' questioning behaviour show that questions constitute 20 to 40 per cent of classroom talk (Chaudron 1988). In most ESL classrooms a major part of classroom interaction is generated by the teacher asking questions. A study of English lessons in schools in Hong Kong found that nearly 70 per cent of classroom talk consists of the teacher asking a question, nominating a student to answer the question, the student answering the question and the teacher providing feedback to the response (Tsui 1985). Questions are therefore a very important aspect of classroom talk.

Questions are usually used to check students' comprehension, to see if they have acquired the knowledge imparted, to focus their attention and involve them in the lesson, to move the lesson forward and, for some teachers, to exercise disciplinary control. In language lessons, questions have the additional function of getting students to practise a certain linguistic item and/or to use the target language to communicate.

2.1.1 Question types

The type of question that the teacher asks affects the kind of response that the students produce. Studies of questioning have proposed various categories of questions, according to such factors as their cognitive demand and their effect on students. In this section we shall consider question types that are important to the analysis of language classrooms.

2.1.2 Open and closed questions

A common way of classifying questions is to look at the question word used: questions that begin with 'what', 'when', 'who' and 'where' are considered 'factual questions' while those that begin with 'how' and 'why' are classified as 'reasoning questions' (Barnes 1969).

ACTIVITY

In order to see whether this classification helps us to understand the nature of questions, compare the 'what' question and the 'how' question in the following text. Would you say that one is a 'factual question' and the other a 'reasoning question'?

2a
(The teacher is discussing a newspaper article about organ transplant with the students.)
T: A heart transplant. Why there was there wasn't a heart transplant? Fanny? Why there wasn't a heart transplant?
F: Because there was no one willing to give a heart to her.
T: Can you hear? Say it louder.
F: Because no one is willing to give a heart to her . . .
T: despite the fact that she had an enormously large heart. The main cause of her death was perhaps she couldn't wait any longer. All right?
(Author's data)

Although the teacher's question begins with 'why', it does not require any reasoning at all. Rather, from the fact that the teacher finishes the sentence for the student, we can see that she expects the student to recall a piece of information from the newspaper article. Therefore, similar to the 'what' question, it is a 'factual question'.

ACTIVITY

Consider now the questions in the following two texts. They both begin with the question word 'what' and they both ask for factual information. But do you notice any difference in the responses that they elicit?

2b

(The teacher is asking students about a story called 'Kee Knock Stan', which means 'I cannot understand'.)

T: *Last week we were reading 'Kee Knock Stan'. What is 'Kee Knock Stan'? Janice.*
S: *I cannot understand.*
T: *Yes. And what language is it supposed to be? Julia.*
S: *Lalloon language.*
T: *Right.*
(Author's data)

2c

(The teacher is asking students about how a post-office worker would sort the mail.)

T: *What do you think the postmen at the post office would do?*
S: *I think I would divide it if the letters are to Hong Kong or other places.*
T: *Yes, I think that's a sensible way, right? Good. All right, now anybody else has any other ideas?*
(Author's data)

From the students' responses and the way the teacher evaluates the responses, we can see that the two questions in **2b** have only one acceptable answer whereas the one in **2c** has a range of acceptable answers. Barnes (1969) refers to the former as 'closed' questions and the latter as 'open' questions. In terms of students' language output, 'closed' questions are more restrictive than 'open' questions. A 'closed' question where the teacher provides the sentence structure as a clue to solicit an appropriate response is even more restrictive. For example:

2d

T: Was he happy? Was he sad? Was he surprised? What did he feel? Pauline.
S: So happy.
T: So happy that he – Venessa.
S: Jumped up.
T: Jumped up. And what else did he do after jumping up? Angel.
(Author's data)

All the pupil is expected to do here is to produce the complement *Jumped up*. While providing clues is an effective way of helping students to arrive at an appropriate answer, we should be aware of the restrictive nature of this kind of blank-filling question in terms of students' language production.

2.1.3 Display and referential questions

In the previous section we saw that the classification of questions into 'open' and 'closed' tells us something about the kind of response elicited. In this section we shall see whether it tells us anything about the nature of the interaction generated by the questions.

ACTIVITY

Compare the 'open', 'factual' question in text **2c** and the two questions in text **2e** below. What are the similarities and differences in the responses that they elicit?

2e
(The teacher is asking the students whether they have dogs at home and what their dogs do when they are happy.)

T: Queenie, when your dog is happy, what does your dog do?
S: He sticks out his tongue.
T: Sticks out his tongue? What does he do when he sticks out his tongue?
S: And wags his tail.
T: And wags his tail. I see. I see he does two things.
(Author's data)

The two questions in text **2e** are similar to that in **2c** in that they all have more than one acceptable answer. However, there is an important difference between the former and the latter. The question in **2c** is one to which the teacher already has the answers. In other words, it is asked not because the teacher wants to know the answers but because the teacher wants to check if the students know the answers. In **2e** the teacher does not have the information and the student answers the questions in order to inform the teacher, rather than to have her answers evaluated as good or bad. These questions are fundamentally different from that in **2c** and those in **2a**, **2b** and **2d**.

Long and Sato (1983) refer to knowledge-checking questions as 'display' questions and those to which the teacher does not have the answer as 'referential' questions. The distinction between 'display' and 'referential' questions is an important one given the emphasis on meaningful communication in the language classroom. To appreciate the difference between kinds of communication generated by these two types of question, consider the exchanges in texts **2f** and **2g** below.

2f
(In the classroom)
T: What's the time?
S: Ten o'clock.
T: Well done.

2g
(At the bus-stop)
Passenger A: What's the time?

Passenger B: Ten o'clock.
Passenger A: Well done.

The exchange in **2g** is odd because, in social communication, people do not generally go around asking questions to which they already have an answer. If they did, challenge or aggression is implied.

In addition to the fact that the questioner genuinely wants to know the answer in social communication, the meaning of an utterance is also subject to negotiation between the speaker and the hearer. Consider the following piece of conversation:

2h

C: Do you get anything knocked off if you're late?
B: No, you get an apology announcement at Victoria Station.
C: No, I mean at work, do you get anything knocked off your wages?
B: Oh. No.
(Tsui 1989: 555)

C's question is misunderstood by B. C, instead of evaluating the answer as wrong, clarifies the meaning of his question, which in turn is responded to appropriately by B. In other words, the meaning of C's question is <u>negotiated</u> between the two speakers. In this case C sticks to the intended meaning of his question and rectifies B's misinterpretation; in other cases the speaker may choose not to rectify misinterpretations, hence changing the intended meaning of their question.

This kind of negotiation of meaning is often absent in the classroom. The meaning of the teacher's question and what constitutes an appropriate answer is usually predetermined by the teacher. If the student's response does not match what the teacher considers to be appropriate, it will be negatively evaluated.

To summarize, 'display' questions generate interactions that are typical of didactic discourse, whereas 'referential' questions generate interactions typical of social communication.

2.1.4 Interpretation of 'display' and 'referential' questions

ACTIVITY

Given the classification of questions into 'display' and 'referential' questions, consider the following piece of classroom conversation. Do you think the teacher has asked a 'display' question or a 'referential' question?

2i

(The teacher has just finished teaching the camping adventure of a group of boys.)

T: *Do you think that, um, was it exciting that night? Mm? Do you think that it was very it was exciting? Right, Chi-ming. What do you think? It was, it was –*

S: *It was very exciting.*

T: *It was very exciting. Right. Yes. Sit down.*

(Tsui 1985: 19)

The teacher appears to be asking for the student's opinion of the story, hence a 'referential question'. However, when we look at the clue that the teacher provides – *It was, it was* – and her evaluation of the student response as correct, we know that in fact the teacher expected the student to say *It was exciting*, which is the concluding sentence in the story. It is therefore a 'display' question.

The student in text **2i** was able to see through the disguise of a 'referential question' and produce the 'appropriate' answer. Sometimes students are unable to do that, and their perfectly appropriate answer may be rejected by the teacher. Sometimes the converse happens in the classroom, particularly in the language classroom, as here:

2j

(The teacher is teaching the linguistic forms 'Have you got – ?' and 'Yes, I have.')

T: *Have you got any brothers and sisters, Pedro?*

S: Yes, I have.
T: You have, good. How many?
S: er no er I no . . .
(Long 1975: 213)

The student, Pedro, takes the teacher's 'referential question' as a 'display question' to practise the taught linguistic forms. It is only when the teacher follows up the question with *How many?* that he realizes the first question was intended to be a 'referential question'.

To summarize, the kinds of question asked have important effects on student responses and the kinds of interaction generated. Teachers who often ask 'display questions' and/or disguise them as 'referential questions' are likely to encourage students to regurgitate facts or pre-formulated language items, and discourage students from trying to communicate their own ideas in the target language. Teachers who often ask 'closed' questions are likely to restrict students' language output. Those who use what appear to be 'open' questions and yet who are not prepared to accept any other answers except those they have in mind will encourage students to guess <u>what they want</u> as an answer rather than <u>what is appropriate</u> as an answer.

2.2 Explanation

Explanation takes up a very significant part of teacher talk, and, given that the role of the teacher is to make knowledge accessible to students, it is surprising how little research has been done on explanation. In the classroom one can make a rough distinction between procedural explanation and content explanation. The former refers to explanation regarding the organizational aspect of the lesson, for example when the teacher explains how an activity should be conducted or gives instructions about homework. The latter refers to the explanation of the subject content of the lesson.

In the language classroom, content explanation refers to the explanation of vocabulary, texts, grammar rules, and so on. In this section we shall focus on content explanation, especially vocabulary and grammar explanation, since they are most frequently found in language classrooms.

2.2.1 Effective explanations

Brown and Armstrong provide a working definition of 'explaining' as 'an attempt to provide understanding of a problem to others' (1984: 122). In other words, it is important to consider how the problem is explained in relation to the audience. As Martin (1970) points out, 'If the teacher really has explained something to his class, they will understand it, and if they do not understand it, despite his efforts, what purported to be an explanation was not an explanation after all.' Hence, in determining whether an explanation is effective, one needs to take into consideration the explainer, the problem to be explained and the person(s) to whom the problem is explained.

Brown and Armstrong (1984) studied the explanations of twenty-seven student-teachers teaching two sessions of ten minutes on a biology topic. Students were asked to complete a content multiple-choice test and a rating form of the student-teacher. The results show that better explanations have the following characteristics:

— higher levels of cognitive demand;
— more linked statements (referred to as 'keys') leading to a solution of the problem, each of which is understood by the students;
— more framing statements outlining the sections of the explanation;
— more focusing statements highlighting the essential features;
— more frequent use of examples, audiovisual aids;
— more rhetorical questions as attention-getters.

They also found that the differences between high-scoring and low-scoring lessons lie in the selection of materials, that is, determining how much needs to be explained, and the presentation of the materials. In the high-scoring lesson the teacher went from known to unknown, whereas in the low-scoring lesson the teacher went from unknown to unknown.

From the findings of Brown and Armstrong's study we can see that the following are important aspects of effective explanation:

— Effective explanation is not a one-way process, involving only the teacher imparting knowledge to students; it requires the active involvement of the students in processing the information and in relating new information to old information.

— It requires that the teacher have a good grasp of the nature of the problem to be explained, so that a set of linked statements (or 'keys') can be presented or elicited from students and the essential features highlighted.

— In order to determine the appropriate amount of new information and the appropriate presentation of the information, the teacher needs to gauge the existing knowledge of the students so that the problem is not over-explained or under-explained (Chaudron 1982).

— The teacher needs to be able to organize the explanation in a clear sequence and to signpost the sequence.

In 2.2.2 and 2.2.3 below we shall examine some data on vocabulary and grammar explanation in the light of the characteristics of effective explanation outlined above.

2.2.2 Grammar explanation

ACTIVITY

Examine the following piece of classroom conversation in which the teacher explains the grammatical mistakes in a sentence. Would you consider this an effective explanation? Does it contain the characteristics of effective explanation?

2k

(This is an S5 (Grade 11) ESL class. The teacher is going over the grammatical mistakes that students made in their writing assignment. Immediately preceding this excerpt he was discussing the error in the sentence 'So I think all students should be learn how to use computers.' He pointed out to the students that an infinitive should be used after a modal verb, so that 'should be learn' ought to be corrected as 'should learn'. He then moved on to the next error.)

1 *T: You can write programmes, play a game, doing calculations,*
2   *drawing a picture, etc. I like the idea very much, you've got some*
3   *concrete examples, but it's not quite balanced so far as grammar*
4   *goes. OK, what is the modal in that sentence?*
5 *Ss: Can.*
6 *T: Can, OK, and we see here the modal* (points at the previous
7   sentence on the board), *now what's the infinitive after should?*
8   (pause) *What's the infinitive after should in this sentence?*
9 *Ss: Learn.*
10 *T: Learn, this is the infinitive. Should learn. If you've got one modal*
11   *in a sentence, all the verbs which follow must be infinitives. So*
12   *pick up your pencils and correct this sentence. First of all, let's*
13   *find the verbs. Which are the verbs?*
14 *Ss: Write, play, doing, drawing.*
15 *T: Write, play, doing, drawing. OK.* (Students correct the errors.)
16   *OK, what did you change?* (pause) *What have you changed*
17   *there?* (pause) *Do I change play?*
18 *Ss: No.*
19 *T: No. Do I change doing?*
20 *Ss: Yes.*
21 *T: Cross out – ?*
22 *Ss: ing.*
23 *T: What about drawing?*
24 *Ss: ing.*
25 *T: Yes, same thing. OK, that's good. You can see now how it*
26   *works. You can have many different verbs following just one*

27   *modal, but they must all be infinitives. Now there's something*
28   *else that needs fixing up. Can anyone suggest what's wrong?*
(Author's data)

The problem to be explained to the students is the use of the infinitive after the modal verb even when there are many different verbs following just one modal verb. We can identify the following characteristics of effective explanation in the excerpt: Firstly, the teacher tries to relate this grammar rule to students' existing knowledge, which is the use of the infinitive after a modal verb, and he actively involves students in doing so. Secondly, the questions that he puts to the students are 'keys', in that they are linked questions that elicit responses leading to the solution of the problem. He first establishes that the students know what a modal verb is by asking *what is the modal in that* (the sentence under discussion) *sentence?* This followed by *What's the infinitive after <u>should</u> in this* (the previous sentence discussed) *sentence?* He then states the rule and tries to get the students to apply it. In applying the rule, he gets the students to identify what the verbs are in the sentence under discussion by asking *Which are the verbs?* Then he goes over each verb and asks them to produce the infinitive form of the verb (lines 17–25). Thirdly, by asking students these key questions, the teacher is actively involving them in processing the new information. Fourthly, the explanation is clearly structured with framing moves like *First of all, let's find the verb*, with a summarizing statement reiterating the rule before he moves on to the next point, thus clearly signposting the end of one teaching sequence and the beginning of another (lines 25–28).

ACTIVITY

Examine the following piece of data and try to answer the following questions:
— Does the teacher try to relate new information to student's existing knowledge?

— Is there active involvement of students?
— Has the teacher used linked statements or questions?
— What other means has the teacher used to help her to explain?
— Has the teacher structured her explanation clearly?

21

(The teacher is teaching the difference between 'after' and 'while' as linkers for joining two actions. She puts a picture on the board. She deals with two points when joining two actions in a sentence: firstly, the duration of the action, and secondly, the tense used.)

1 T: Now step back and look at it again. Go back to think about
2   things which happened in the morning. Now here you've got two
3   interesting points. First of all, he turned on the tap and then the
4   telephone rang. Now, do you think you can join them together?
5   The two events, they have certain causal relationships. So how
6   do you join the two events together?
7 S: While the telephone rang. When he was –
8 T: OK, right. Look at it again. Look at the picture again. Now see
9   what actually happened.
10 S1: After he turned on the bath, he heard the telephone ring.
11 S2: While.
12 T: Now here we've got two people, Sam and Wilfred, using two
13   different words to join them together. One is the word _while_.
14   Sam used _while_ to join them together. Wilfred used the other
15   word and that is _after_. Is there any difference between these
16   words? _While_?
17 Ss: _While_, happening at the same time.
18 T: _While_, happening –?
19 Ss: At the same time.
20 T: OK. You used _while_ when the two things are supposed to be
21   happening at the same time. What about _after_?
22 S: One follow the other.
23 T: OK, one follow another. So two events, one following the other.
24   Now look at the picture again. Which is true?
25 S: _After_ (pause)

26 T: *The second one is right. Do you agree?*

27 S: *Yes.*

28 T: *Now why?*

29 S: *Because in fact the telephone rang after he turned on.*

30 T: *Yes.*

31 S: *Then Henry was working, walking, to the phone.*

32 T: *Yes. Right. Do you agree, Sam? Because the action of turning*

33   *on the tap is a very short one. Think about the action itself. It's*

34   *a very short one. You turned on the tap, the telephone rang.*

35   *Now, but suppose if I don't use the verb turned on the tap, I use*

36   *another verb. If I say run a bath, what would you use?*

37 S: *The first one.*

38 T: *The first one? OK. Give me the complete sentence.*

39 S: *While Henry was running a bath, the telephone rang.*

40 T: *So you would say While Henry was running a bath, the telephone*

41   *rang. Do you agree, the rest of you? Think about that. What's*

42   *the difference?*

43 S: *The action.*

44 T: *What about the action?*

45 S: *Running a bath would take a long time.*

46 T: *Yeah. Do you agree? Running a bath would take a very long*

47   *time . . .*

(Author's data)

In lines 10 and 11 there are two competing answers to the teachers' questions of how to join the two events. In response to that, the teacher activates students' knowledge of the words 'while' and 'after' (lines 12–23). She then refers to the picture and asks students to decide which one is correct; there is active cognitive involvement of students. Apart from asking questions the teacher also asks students to give reasons for or explain their answers (lines 28, 41–42, 44). In trying to explain that, when joining two events together, we need to look at the duration of the event, she asks the following linked questions: *Is there any difference between these words* (that is, 'while' and 'after')? *While? What about after?, Now look at the picture again. Which is true, Why?, If I say* <u>run a bath</u>*, what would you use?, What's the difference?,* and *What about the action?* Apart from verbal presentation, she uses pictures to help her. At various points in the explanation she draws students' attention to the picture to help them come up with the correct answers to her questions (lines 8, 24). Finally, the teacher signposts the explanation. She uses focusing moves such as *Now step back and look at it again. Go back to think about things which happened in the morning, Look at the picture again,* and *Now look at the picture again,* and framing moves such as *Now here you've got two interesting points.*

2.2.3 Vocabulary explanation

Vocabulary explanation is found in all language classrooms, whether L1 or L2. While there is no lack of study on vocabulary learning not many have focused on vocabulary explanation.

Similar to grammar explanation, effective vocabulary explanation requires that the teacher be able to gauge accurately students' competence level, in order to decide how elaborate the explanation needs to be, as well as the existing knowledge of the students, in order to relate new and old information, to highlight the essential features of the item to be explained and to actively involve students in processing the meaning of words. In the ensuing discussion we shall examine some classroom data according to these aspects.

Lee (1993b) studied vocabulary explanation of ESL teachers. In the first part of her study she identified the explanation strategies used by teachers by examining four reading comprehension lessons taught by four ESL teachers at S3 and S4 (Grades 14 and 15). In the second part of the study she tested out the effectiveness of these strategies by teaching ten vocabulary items to four groups of ESL students at S3 (Grade 9) in the same school, using different strategies, and comparing their pre-test and post-test scores. She observed that decisions regarding which vocabulary item to explain and how best to explain it necessarily involves the teacher's judgement of the competence of the students. For example, one of the teachers used exemplification to explain eight out of eleven vocabulary items; and for seven of these eight items she used one example. But for the eighth item, which is the most difficult item – 'sophistication' – she used two examples:

2m

T: When we say sophisticated, we mean em something which is highly developed, for example, these two tape recorders, I think they are quite sophisticated. They've got a lot of functions, all right? And also, sometimes we can use this word to describe a person. A person who is sophisticated, that means a person who has a lot of knowledge, very experienced with things, right? A sophisticated machine, very well done, OK? Now can you do this together? Sophisticated.

(Lee 1993b: 45)

However, Lee also found that an inaccurate estimation of students' competence may lead to under-teaching or over-teaching. In the explanation of one of the vocabulary items – 'initiative' – she found that while nine students in Group Two got the meaning correct, only one student in Group One got it correct.

ACTIVITY

Examine the two texts below, in which the teacher explains the word 'initiative'. Which do you think occurred in Group One and which in Group Two?

2n

T: Now, initiative comes from the word initiate. To initiate means to start something. If you start something, then you initiate something. So if you show initiative in something, that means you don't have to wait for people to tell you what to do. You can start doing something on your own. That is to show er initiative in your work, OK? Now, for example, if you if you are a good student you should show initiative in lear- learning. You don't have to wait for the teacher to tell you what to do and what to read. You can do things on your own, OK? You know when you should finish your homework, when you start your revision, you know when to go to the library and borrow books and learn more about a subject, all right? To show initiative, all right? You can do things on your own. You can start working on your own without waiting, without having to wait to be told what to do.

(Lee 1993b)

2o

T: Er, initiative means er that means if you have if you take the initiative to do something, that means you don't have to wait for people to tell you what to do. You can do things on your own without waiting for people to tell you what to do, OK? You don't have to wait for people to tell you, you can do that before people tell you what to do.

(Lee 1993b)

In text **2n** the teacher (who was Lee herself) paraphrased the meaning of 'initiative' and gave an example to help students come to grips with the meaning, in the first paragraph. Lee pointed out that she was afraid the example was not sufficient, and so she carried on a few more lines and gave a list of what a good student with initiative would do, like finishing homework, starting revision, and going to the library to find out more about a subject. This, however, caused confusion rather than helping to clarify the meaning, as only one student got the meaning correct. By contrast, in text **2o** the teacher (who was also Lee herself) paraphrased the meaning of 'initiative', and then repeated the paraphrase without even giving an example – yet nine students got the meaning correct. In other words, over-elaborate explanation may cause confusion.

Lee also observed that effective explanations were those where the teacher was able to relate what the students were familiar with to the item being explained. For example, in the following excerpt the teacher explains the word 'convenient'. She relates the word to 7-Eleven stores, which were referred to as 'convenience stores' in television commercials.

2p

T: *OK, convenient transportation, transportation system. 7-Eleven You're finished? If you're finished, please put down your pen. 7-Eleven, you know 7-Eleven? is a convenience store, is a convenience store. Why? Because it opens*

   [

Ss: *Yes.*

T: *how many hours a day? 24 hours.*

                   [

Ss: *24 hours.*

T: *In other words, you can go to the store any time you want. So it's very convenient for the neighbourhood, OK? So you can say um 7-Eleven is a convenience store. Convenient, all right? Understand convenient? . . .*

(Lee 1993b)

Other commonly used ways of relating the unfamiliar to the familiar and unknown to known are using examples, putting the word in a familiar context, providing the parts of speech of the same word that students already know, or analysing the morphological structure of the word so that students can go from the familiar part(s) of the word to the unfamiliar part(s).

ACTIVITY

The following are two explanations of the word 'ambitions' given to two groups of students in Lee's study. Which do you think is more effective?

2q

T: *Now ambitions are things you want to be or you want to do. Well, like for example, when I was a small girl, my ambition was to be – what? No not a teacher, was to be an animal doctor, OK? Have you got any ambitions?* (to a student) *What is your ambition?*

S: *Nurse.*

T: *You want to be a nurse* (to another student) *Yours? Yes, you. Yes, have you got any ambitions?* (Ss laugh) *Nothing?* (to another student) *You.*

S: *A teacher.*

T: *To be a teacher. OK. Ambitions, repeat, ambitions.*

Ss: *Ambitions.*

T: *All right.*

(Lee 1993b)

2r

T: *You know what ambitions are? Em ambitions are things you want to be or things you want to do. OK? Ambitions.*

Ss: *Ambitions.*

T: *Ambitions.*

Ss: *Ambitions.*

(Lee 1993b)

In both texts the teacher gives a definition of the word 'ambitions' and gets the students to repeat the word after her. However, in **2q** the teacher not only gives an example to illustrate what 'ambition' means but also involves the students in getting them to state what their ambitions are. By contrast, in **2r** the teacher merely presents a definition of 'ambitions'. And in comparing the pre-test and post-test scores, Lee found that ten students in **2q** were able to give the correct meaning in the post-test whereas in **2r** only one student got the correct meaning in the post-test. Active involvement of students in processing new information, as in **2q**, is very important in effective vocabulary explanation. This is supported by studies in vocabulary learning (Nation 1990).

2.3 Feedback and error treatment

2.3.1 Teacher feedback

Another very important aspect of teacher talk is providing feedback to student responses. It is in the feedback that teachers make evaluations of and give comments on students' performance. This can be seen from the fact that classroom exchanges typically consist of three parts: an initiation from the teacher, a response from the student, followed by a feedback from the teacher. Teacher feedback is so much part of the classroom interaction routine that, when it is absent after a student response, students know that there must be something wrong or unsatisfactory about the response. For example:

2s

T: Now can you change that sentence to 'they'? Instead of saying he runs quickly, can you change that sentence to 'they'? Queenie?

S: They runs they runs quickly.

T: Once more.

S: They run quickly.

T: Yes, that's better.

(Author's data)

After the first student response the teacher, instead of evaluating it, asks the student to give the response once again. That the student realizes the response is unsatisfactory can be seen from the fact that, instead of giving an exact repetition of the response, she gives one with the error corrected. The teacher then accepts the response as an improvement on the previous one. Withholding feedback until a correct response is produced is a common strategy used by teachers to avoid giving negative evaluation.

2.3.2 Affective aspect of teacher feedback

The kind of feedback that a teacher provides affects student learning. A teacher who constantly provides negative feedback is bound to create a sense of failure and frustration among students, and will inhibit student contribution. On the other hand, a teacher who values every contribution and provides encouraging feedback is much more likely to get students motivate to learn and to participate in class, and will help to create a warm social climate in the classroom. As Krashen (1982, 1983) points out, students must be favourably disposed towards language learning before language acquisition will take place.

Teacher feedback is usually associated with evaluating and providing information related to student responses, but these are not the only functions. Teacher feedback can also acknowledge the information that students offers or provide personal comments on students response.

Since one of the major functions of teacher feedback is to evaluate students' performance, in the rest of this section we shall examine closely the area of error correction, or error treatment.

2.3.3 What is an error?

An error in the classroom is commonly understood as something that is rejected by the teacher because it is wrong or inappropriate. However, when classroom exchanges are examined it is found that what teachers consider to be errors may not be wrong or inappropriate at all.

Firstly, an error may be something that the teacher does not want. For example:

2t

*T: Now can you make another sentence with another verb 'swim'?
Eva.*

S: I am swimming.
T: I don't want 'swimming'. I want 'swim'.
(Author's data)

The student produces a perfectly correct response, using the verb specified by the teacher. Prior to this exchange, some students were making sentences with verbs in present continuous tense and some in simple present tense. There is no instruction from the teacher that the student is to use the simple present tense. In other words, the response is rejected by the teacher simply because it is not what she wants.

Secondly, an error may be something that does not conform to the rules that the teacher lays down. For example:

2u

T: Who were hungry? Who were hungry? (nominates)
S: They were hungry.
T: They? Don't use the pronoun. Don't use the pronoun.
S: The boys were all hungry.
T: The boys were all hungry.
(Author's data)

The teacher previously laid down a rule that, when answering questions, pronouns should not be used. The student's response is rejected not because the referent *they* is not specified but because it does not follow the rule that she has set down. Similarly, other correct answers may be rejected because they do not conform to rules or protocol (such as putting a hand up before answering or always replying in complete sentences), or because they do not follow a teacher's idiosyncratic perception of what is linguistically correct. This latter kind of error correction can have an undesirable effect on students' perception of how the target language works.

2.3.4 Errors and language development

While errors made in the language classroom are often frowned upon by teachers and corrected, 'errors' made by children in learning their first language are seldom treated in this manner. Parents and caretakers attend to the message that the child is trying to get across rather than its form. If a child utters the words 'mummy socks', asking his mummy to give him his socks, the mother will expand the utterance into 'Yes, mummy will give you your socks' rather than telling the child that there is an error in the form or that he ought to put it in a complete sentence. This kind of elaboration serves as language input to the child, who will, through constant exposure, acquire the correct form.

Studies in first-language acquisition have pointed out that very often the so-called 'errors' made by children are manifestations of the hypotheses that they are constantly testing out about the language they are trying to master. One often quoted example is 'overgeneralization' in the acquisition of past tense forms. A child may have used the form 'went' as the past tense of 'go' for several months and suddenly switch to 'goed'. This 'error' is the result of the child trying to apply the past tense rule to all verbs. In other words, instead of treating 'goed' as simply an error that is undesirable and should be got rid of as soon as possible, it should be seen as indicative of the stage of language development that the child is in.

Similarly, in second-language learning, students go through a process of hypothesis testing. For example, in an ESL lesson in Hong Kong a student put a sentence on the board that read 'Bus is shorter than the M.T.R.' (M.T.R. stands for Mass Transit Railway, which is the only one in Hong Kong). The teacher put an upright arrow in front of the word 'bus' to show that something was missing. One of the students said that the indefinite article 'a' should be added. Another student, however, said it should be 'A bus is shorter than a M.T.R.'. The second student is clearly making a generalization about the use of an indefinite article in front of the two nouns since they are both public transportation vehicles.

The errors that are made in the process of acquiring a native language or a second language have been referred to as 'developmental errors'. A developmental view of errors sees 'errors' not as something undesirable but as something that informs the teacher about the students' stage of language development.

2.3.5 Should errors be corrected?

To most language teachers the answer to the above question is quite obvious: of course errors should be corrected, or else students would think that what they have produced is correct and will carry on using these erroneous forms. Furthermore, the erroneous output may also cause other students to internalize these errors, or to change their correct hypotheses about the target language to accommodate these incorrect forms. This view that errors should be corrected is shared not only by teachers but also by learners. Cathcart and Olsen (1976) conducted a survey of 149 adult learners and a strong preference for correction of all errors was found. However, when learners were actually corrected intensively, they did not like it.

ACTIVITY

Consider the following conversation. This an ESL classroom and the students are very reticent. Their English is very weak. The teacher corrects every error. Would you do the same if you were in her position?

2v

T: *What did they do after their wonderful meal? What did they do after their wonderful meal? What did they do after their wonderful meal? Chi Hang.*

S: They told stories and sing songs by the –

T: Sing song? Pay attention. Once again. Not sing song, past tense please.

S: They told story and sung song.

T: Sung? No.

S: Sang song.

T: Once again.

S: They told story and sing song.

T: No.

S: They told story and sang song by the fire.

T: They told story and sang song by the fire.

(Author's data)

The student is able to produce a response that is correct in terms of content the first time round. However, because the teacher wants him to correct every single error, he struggles to meet the teacher's demand. What is obvious from the data is that the teacher's expectation of an error-free sentence is far too high. While the student seems to be able to produce the correct form when the sentence is taken apart and dealt with in segments, he does not seem able to do so when the sentence is taken as a whole. In other words, it is beyond the student's capability to produce an error-free sentence containing two verbs in the past tense form. What is ironical is that, after painstakingly correcting the errors, the student's last sentence, which is <u>not</u> error-free, is accepted by the teacher without correcting the error.

The consequence of correcting every error in this particular case is that the student will have no sense of achievement despite the fact that he knows the answer to the teacher's question, and he is likely to be discouraged from answering questions in the future. As studies in error treatment have pointed out, in circumstances where students do not seem to have reached a stage in interlanguage development where they will benefit from the corrective feedback provided by the teacher, the best thing for the teacher to do is to ignore the error (Allwright and Bailey 1991).

In other words, the question of whether errors should be corrected depends on the language competence of the students. It also depends on the kind of students we are teaching. For students with low language proficiency it would be unreasonable to expect error-free sentences. For students who are very shy and reticent it is more important to get them to express themselves rather than to produce correct forms.

ACTIVITY

Consider now the following two pieces of classroom conversation. Do you think the student's errors ought to be corrected in each case?

2w

T: *What is the lesson in this story? What did you learn from the story? Anyone who can tell me?*

S: *Care to choose the friend.*

T: *Steven, repeat your answer again loudly.*

S: *Mm, choose someone's friend more carefully.*

T: *Choose someone's friend more carefully. How? How should you be careful? What kind of friend should you choose?*

S: *Careful and friendly.*

T: *Careful?*

S: *Helpful.*

T: *Helpful? Helpful. Right. Helpful and friendly.*

(Author's data)

2x

T: *Why did she think she had done something wrong? Can I ask one person to answer my question? Venessa, can you answer the question? OK?*

V: *Because she can't* (/kɑːnt/)

T: *Because she counted –*

V: *Because she counted the wrong number of the tourists.*

T: *She counted the wrong number of tourists. Why? Why did she count the wrong number?*

V: *She distr-*

T: *She was distracted by what?*

V: *By the tourists.*

T: *By one of the tourists.*

V: *Which bought a /hʌndz/ vase.*

T: *Huge vase from an an-*

V: *Antique shop.*

(Author's data)

In text **2w** the student's response is not so much linguistically incorrect as semantically incorrect; to choose friends who are *careful and friendly* does not make much sense. The teacher therefore questions the word *careful*, which is then revised to *helpful* by the student. This correction, which the teacher helps the student to make, renders the response meaningful. In text **2x** the first error is one of pronunciation, which is corrected by the teacher. If the student had been allowed to finish the sentence she would have produced a sentence that says *She /kɑːnt/ the wrong number of tourists*, and the hearers would still have been able to understand the message. However, if the second pronunciation error were not corrected the hearers would not be able to understand the message. In other words, while some errors may mar communication, others will not. Hence, another dimension in deciding whether errors should be corrected is the nature of the error. If the error significantly hinders communication, then correction is necessary.

Yet another dimension that is taken into consideration by teachers is the focus of the lesson. Several studies on error correction show that if the focus of the lesson is on form, then teachers are more likely to correct errors related to linguistic form, as well as those that hinder communication. However, when the focus is on content, errors that do not hinder communication often go uncorrected. It is important to distinguish whether the focus is on accuracy or fluency; to correct both form and content errors will be too inhibiting for students.

It should be noted that the correction of an error by the teacher does not necessarily prevent the error occurring again. Allwright and Bailey (1991: 99) use the terms 'treatment' and 'cure' to distinguish between the teacher's correcting the error and the student's acquiring the correct form, and they point out that they are not the same thing.

2.3.6   Immediate and delayed treatment of errors

Once the teacher has decided that an error should be treated, the next decision that he or she has to make is when to treat the error: should it be treated immediately or should the treatment be delayed? In text **2x** above, we have an example of error treatment that is given immediately, by interrupting the student in the middle of the sentence. The problem with immediate treatment is that it is disruptive. A student whose response or contribution is constantly being interrupted may find it very frustrating and inhibiting. Therefore, a teacher may decide to delay treatment until the student finishes whatever he or she wants to say.

Sometimes a teacher may decide to point out an error but postpone the treatment until later in the lesson. Teachers may postpone treatment for an even longer period of time, that is, beyond the limit of a lesson. As Allwright and Bailey (1991) point out, if the errors are patterned and are shared by a group of students, the teacher may use these errors as a starting-point for a future lesson. Long (1977: 290) observes that error treatment becomes less effective as the time lag between the performance and the treatment becomes bigger. However, the effectiveness of immediate and delayed error treatment is an area that still needs to be researched.

2.3.7 How errors are corrected

The last stage in the decision-making process is determining how errors are to be corrected. This involves the question of who corrects the errors and the way in which they are corrected. The teacher can decide to correct them, to get the student who produced the error to correct them, or to get other students to do so.

If the teacher decides to correct the error, he or she can repeat the student's response with correction. This kind of modelling can be very effective because it avoids providing explicit negative evaluation and exposes students to the correct form. Sometimes students are then able to pick up the correct form, as here:

2y
T: *What is the reason?*
S: *Because he can play tennis and also the ping-pong ball, also drive the sports and mm he can <u>speak the German</u>.*
T: *He can <u>speak German</u>, and how about the girl?*
S: *The girl can also <u>speak German</u>, yes.*
(Author's data)

However, we must be careful not to conclude that the student has acquired the correct form, because it is possible that the production of the correct form is short-lived and has not been internalized.

The teacher can also deal with errors directly, with explanation. For example:

2z
T: *Now can you find a noise, a word which shows a noise?*
Ss: *(bid)*
T: *Queenie.*
S: *Pattering.*
T: *Right. The pattering paw-steps of one stray dog. Another one?*
Ss: *(bid)*
T: *Yes?*
S: *Flutter.*

T: Flutter. But fluttering isn't a lot of noise, because when a leaf falls it turns round and round in the wind but it doesn't really make a noise, does it? So fluttering is hardly a noise at all, but paw-steps, pitter patter pitter patter quietly. So it means the place is very quiet. All right?

(Author's data)

If the teacher decides to get the student to self-correct, then the teacher can point out to the students the presence of an error, the location of an error or the identity of an error (Long 1977). The presence of an error can be indicated implicitly or explicitly. An example of the former would be the teacher withholding acceptance or acknowledgement of the student response. Another example is simply asking the student to repeat his or her own utterance. Text **2w** above contains examples of both methods.

The teacher may indicate the location of an error by repeating the error with a rising intonation. He or she could also explicitly indicate the location; for example:

2aa
T: After they have put up their tent, what did the boys do?
S: They cooking food.
T: No, not they cooking food, pay attention.
S: They cook their meal.
T: Right, they cook their meal over an open fire.
(Author's data)

The teacher could also implicitly indicate the location of the error by asking the student to repeat a certain word or phrase. For example, in text **2aa** above, the teacher, instead of saying *No, not they cooking food*, could have said simply *They – ,* thus implicitly indicating *cooking* as the error.

Finally, a teacher may indicate the nature of the error made. For example, in text **2v** above, the teacher actually tells the student that *sing song* is wrong because the verb should be in past tense form.

The teacher may choose to get other students to correct an error. For example, see text **1h** (p. 15).

So far there is no answer to the question of what kind of error correction is most effective, and perhaps there never will be. This is because, as mentioned earlier, it is the learner who determines whether the correct form is acquired, not the teacher.

PROJECT

Record and transcribe a fifteen-minute segment of a lesson taught by yourself or a colleague, and examine one of the following aspects:

1. Question type and student response: Examine the student responses elicited by different types of question and different combinations of question types. Pay attention to both the quantitative and qualitative aspects of student responses.
2. Vocabulary or grammar explanation: Consider whether you or your colleague i) correctly gauged the competence level of the students, ii) tried to relate new information to students' existing knowledge, iii) actively involved students in processing new information, iv) used a set of linked statements, v) highlighted the essential features, vi) signposted the explanation.
3. Treatment of error: Ask yourself the following questions when examining the data.
   — Were errors corrected? Why and why not?
   — Was the error correction done immediately or was it delayed? Why?
   — How was the error corrected? Was it self-corrected, other-corrected or teacher-corrected? Why?
   — Was the error indicated to the student? If yes, was the nature and/or the location of the error indicated? Why?
   — Was there an explanation of the error? Why?

SUMMARY

● Different types of question affect the kinds of student response

53

elicited, both quantitatively and qualitatively, as well as the kind of learning that takes place.

- Classrooms that are dominated by display questions encourage regurgitation of what the teacher wants rather than creative thinking or creative use of language.
- Effective explanations are those that actively involve learners in processing the new information, that help learners to relate new information to old, that are at the appropriate level and that are well organized.
- Decisions made by the teacher as to whether to correct an error, and how and when to correct it, have important effects on students' learning.

3 Input and interaction

In chapter 2 we examined various aspects of teacher talk and how they affect student response and learning. One very important factor in the effectiveness of teacher talk is whether it is comprehensible to the students. According to Krashen (1977, 1982, 1985), input that is totally incomprehensible to learners is not likely to cause learning to take place.

Early research on teacher talk focused on how teachers modify their own speech in terms of phonology, syntax and lexis. More recent research maintains that modified interaction is more important in terms of students getting comprehensible input.

In this chapter we shall examine various ways in which teachers modify their input to make it comprehensible and the interactional structure generated in the process. We shall also discuss the role of students in obtaining comprehensible input, and their turn-taking behaviour.

3.1 Modified input

Studies on teachers' modified speech have found that there are certain characteristics of ESL teacher talk that differentiate it from social talk. In terms of phonology, teachers tend to slow down their speech rate, and use less reduced vowels, fewer contractions, more standard pronunciation and more exaggerated articulation. In terms of syntax, teachers tend to use better-formed and shorter sentences, and fewer subordinate and conditional clauses. In terms of vocabulary, teacher talk is more basic, with fewer colloquial expressions, more concrete and proper nouns, and fewer indefinite pronouns.

In this section we shall focus on how teachers modify their questions in order to make them more comprehensible.

3.1.1 Modification of questions

It is fairly common among teachers to simply repeat a question when they fail to get a response from students. Tsui (1985) found that up to 86.5 per cent of an ESL teacher's questions were repetitions of the previous question. While verbatim repetition has its place in helping students to process the question, particularly for those with low English proficiency, it is important for teachers to remember that, when a response is not forthcoming even after it is repeated verbatim, the question needs to be modified.

Generally speaking we may say that there are two kinds of question modification; one is comprehension-oriented and the other is response-oriented. The former makes the question easier for the students to understand, whereas the latter makes it easier for the students to respond to.

3.1.2 Comprehension-oriented modifications

3.1.2.1 Syntactical modification

ACTIVITY

Examine the following conversation from a Primary Four ESL classroom. What kind of modification has the teacher made to her question?

3a
T: Do you know what an emperor is? What is an emperor? Joyce.
S: A man who ruled the country.
T: Yes.
(Author's data)

The teacher's initial question is an embedded question. What the teacher wants the student to tell her is what an emperor is, not whether or not she knows what an emperor is. The embedding of *What is an emperor?* in another question makes it difficult for students to understand. The teacher therefore modifies the syntax by disembedding the question to which the teacher wishes the students to respond. Long (1983b) refers to this kind of syntactical modification as 'making the topic salient'.

3.1.2.2 Semantic modification

Syntactic structure is not the only source of difficulty. In text **2b** below, the teacher, upon getting no response, modifies the syntax of her original question by getting rid of the hypothetical clause. Yet she still fails to get a response.

3b

T: *I suppose if you were on the street and somebody comes up to you and says to you we – can you tell me the way to a certain theatre, maybe you would, but maybe you wouldn't even. But if somebody says can you tell me who designed that building, would you know?*

Ss: (silence)

T: *Do you know who designed any building at all?*

Ss: (silence)

T: *Do you know the name of any architect who designs buildings in Hong Kong at all?*

S: (bid)

T: *Yes?*

S: *My father is an architect.*

(Tsui 1992: 55)

As soon as the teacher modifies the lexical items *who* and *any building* to *the name of any architect* and *buildings in Hong Kong* respectively, a student volunteers to answer the question and tells the teacher that her father is an architect. By asking students *who*, the teacher gives the impression that the answer should be a specific person; when she modifies it to *the name of any architect*, the acceptability of a range of answers becomes clear. By contrast, *any building* causes difficulty because it has no specific referent; and when the teacher modifies it to *buildings in Hong Kong*, the referents are narrowed down and the question becomes easier to answer. In other words, the teacher has made semantic modifications to the question at the lexical level.

It is particularly important to make the referent clear when giving instructions. Students who missed the referent would find themselves not being able to make sense of the rest of what the teacher says.

ACTIVITY

Examine the following text. How does the teacher modify her question? Why do you think she modifies it in such a way.

3c

T: So that's a very good descriptive sentence. It tells you exactly what the dog looks like. Can you picture the dog? If I were to ask you to draw the dog, would you be able t- to draw the dog?

Ss: Yes, yes.

(Author's data)

The word *picture* in the teacher's initial question means 'imagine' or 'make a mental representation'. The teacher modifies it into something more concrete and familiar to students, namely, whether they would be able to draw the dog. This kind of lexical modification is commonly used by teachers when they realize they have used a word that may be too difficult or abstract for their students.

Sometimes the teacher may paraphrase what they have said not because the words used are too difficult but because they are vague. Take the following piece of data for example:

3d

T: (draws a dog on the blackboard) *Is this <u>the right picture</u> to draw? Is this <u>what the dog would look like</u>?*

Ss: *No.*

T: *No, because this one has an ear standing up. It looks more like a horse head than a dog head but you know it's got floppy ears, the ears hang down like that. Right?*

(Author's data)

The teacher has drawn a picture of a dog on the blackboard according to the description in the story-book, which says 'He was a shabby little dog with a short, rough coat and small floppy ears.' In order to help them understand the meaning of 'floppy ears' she drew the dog with one ear standing up. She then asks the students whether it is the *right picture*. The meaning of the phrase *right picture* could be vague and she modifies it to *what the dog would look like*.

From the above examples we can see that it is very important for teachers to be aware that what is clear to them may not be at all clear to students. Sometimes the meaning of the entire question is not clear. Instead of modifying certain lexical items, the entire question has to be rephrased.

ACTIVITY

Consider the following conversation. Put yourself in the students' shoes. Would you be able to answer the teacher's initial question? Would you be able to answer the modified question? What answer do you think the teacher is looking for.

3e

(The teacher has been asking the students what problems they would come across as a taxi-driver and as a passenger.)

T: *... OK, I'm going to write up something on the board now and I want you to tell me what it is, where you would find this.*

(Teacher writes on the board 'Police to pursue crooked cabbies'.)

T: *Police to pursue crooked cabbies. What IS it? Never mind what it means, but what IS it?*

Ss: (silence – 3.02 seconds)

T: *Where would you find this?*

(Author's data)

The answer the teacher is looking for to the initial question *What IS it?* is 'It's a newspaper headline.' But the question is by no means clear. The modification of the question into *Where would you find this?*, which is intended as a clue to help students answer the question, is even less clear: does it mean where would you find police pursuing crooked cabbies or where would you find lines like this? It is therefore not surprising that, even though the teacher waits longer for a response than to the initial question, he is still unable to get one. Let us see how the teacher handles the interaction:

T: *Police to pursue crooked cabbies. What IS it? Never mind what it means, but what IS it?*

Ss: (silence – 3.02 seconds)

T: *Where would you find this?*

Ss: (silence – 8.57 seconds)

T: *Ricky, how can you tell that that belongs in the newspaper?*

R: (silence – 5.07 seconds) *It is like a headline.*

T: *Yeah, it looks like a headline. You can recognize headlines because there's generally no article. You can't see the article 'the' there can you?*

(Author's data)

We can see that in the second modification the teacher actually gives the answer to the preceding question, *Where would you find this?* By pointing out that it belongs to the newspaper, the scope of the response is narrowed down and the meaning of the initial question, *What IS it?*, becomes clearer.

3.1.3   Response-oriented modification

3.1.3.1   Syntactical modifications

One type commonly used by teachers is a modification of the
syntax from wh- questions to yes–no questions. The following is
an example:

3f

*T: And in the following line, it says 'When the clouds lifted'. What
does it mean there, 'the clouds lifted'? Anasa.*

S: (pause) Had an idea.

*T: He possibly had an idea, yes, that took him out of what? Out of
this particular –*

S: (silence)

T: What sort of mood was he in, Anasa, to begin with?

S: (silence)

T: Was he in a good mood?

S: No.

*T: No, he was in a very bad mood, a black mood, with lots of evil
thoughts, and it was as though there was a cloud over him
because he was feeling so angry.*

(Tsui 1985)

The teacher modifies the wh- question to a yes–no question. This
kind of modification often succeeds in getting a student response
because, firstly, the answer to the question is much narrower; in
this example, the answer to *What mood is he in?* is narrowed down
to a 'good or bad mood'. Secondly, it makes the production of a
response much easier; students only have to answer 'yes' or 'no'. A
cautionary note should be added here: while this kind of modification helps students to produce a response, it is restrictive in terms
of language production; overuse of this kind of modification de-
prives students of the chance to produce longer responses.

3.1.3.2 Lexical modification

Narrowing down possible answers can be achieved not only by syntactical modification but also by lexical modification.

Consider the following piece of classroom conversation. What lexical and syntactical modifications has the teacher made? Do you think the modifications are effective? Why?

3g

T: *First point, taxi-drivers often choose passengers. Where in Hong Kong do you think this would take place?*

Ss: (whispering among themselves)

T: *Pardon?*

Ss: (silence – 3 seconds) *Central.*

T: *Central. OK. Why in Central?*

Ss: (silence – 4.46 seconds)

T: *Why would taxi-drivers choose their passengers in Central?*

Ss: (silence – 6.20 seconds)

T: *Let me put it another way. Why wouldn't a taxi-driver want to take a passenger somewhere?*

Ss: (silence – 6.82 seconds)

T: *Stella.*

S: *Because he doesn't want to take a short journey.*

(Author's data)

The teacher modifies the lexical item *choose* to *want to take*, and the positive question *Why would – ?* to a negative question *Why wouldn't – ?* While the word *choose* embraces the meaning of *want* and *not want*, hence opening up a range of possible answers, the phrase *wouldn't want to take* narrows down the possible answers.

3.1.3.3 Providing clues

Another kind of response-orientated modification is the provision of clues. The clues may be in the form of giving part of the answer and asking students to provide the rest. For example:

3h

T: What would you do if I ask you to blink?
Ss: (blinking their eyes)
T: You're all blinking away? So what are you actually doing? What are you doing? Olivia, what have you been doing? Opening and –
S: Closing.
T: Closing what? your mouth?
Ss: (laugh)
S: My eyes.
T: Your eyes.
(Author's data)

The intention of the teacher's initial question, *What are you doing?* is not clearly conveyed. The logical answer to the question is 'I am blinking my eyes', but it clearly is not what the teacher is looking for. By providing the clue *Opening and –* the teacher makes it clear that she intends the question to mean 'describe what you are physically doing'. (Note, however, the restrictive nature of blank-filling questions. See section 2.1.2.)

Another way of giving students a clue would be to provide a possible answer to the question in order to lead students to think of other possibilities.

3.1.3.4 Socratic questioning

A fourth type of modification is the Socratic questioning type in which, when students fail to respond, the teacher asks a series of questions that finally leads to the answer to the initial question. For example:

3i

The teacher is discussing the tense in the headline 'Police to pursue crooked cabbies'.

T: *But generally in the newspaper, if it were going to be past tense, they would use a past tense. So the police – if that were past tense, what would they say?*

Ss: (silence)

T: *What's the past tense of pursue?*

Ss: (silence)

T: *What what letters do I add to the end of pursue to make it past tense?*

Ss: *ed.*

T: *ed. OK, so it would be 'Police pursued crooked cabbies'.*

(Author's data)

The teacher is trying to help students to answer the initial question by going from general to specific. He goes from the general question of what the headline would be if it were in the past tense, to focusing on the past tense form of the verb 'pursue', to narrowing down the possible answer to the past tense form of regular verbs, which only requires the addition of 'ed'. In other words, rather than modifying the syntax or the semantics of the question, the teacher narrows down the answer by asking a series of leading questions.

3.2 Modified interaction

As mentioned at the beginning of this chapter, recent studies of classroom interaction maintain that modification of the interaction between teacher and students is more crucial to the provision of comprehensible input than modification of teacher talk in terms of grammar and vocabulary. The concept of interactional modification arises from observation of the differences between conversation among native speakers (NSs) and that between NSs and non-native speakers (NNSs). The adjustments that NSs make to enable NNSs to understand what has been said result in different interactional structures. For example:

3j

| NS: | *What time did you finish?* | (question) |
| NS: | *Ten.* | (answer) |

NS:	*When did you finish?*	(question)
NNS:	*Um?* [Uh? sic]	(repetition request)
NS:	*When did you finish?*	(repetition)
NNS:	*Ten clock.*	(answer)
NS:	*Ten o'clock?*	(confirmation check)
NNS:	*Yeah.*	(confirmation)

(Long 1983a:128)

In the first conversation, the interactional structure consists of two 'turns', a question followed by an answer. In the second, however, because the NNS cannot catch the question the first time round, he requests a repetition. After the repetition, the NNS gives an answer. Because there is an error in the answer, the NS asks for confirmation from the NNS that he has understood the answer correctly. This result is an interactional structure consisting of six turns.

3.2.1 Modification devices in interaction

Studies into the modification of interactional structure in NS–NNS conversations have noted that there are a number of devices that native speakers use both to avoid and to repair breakdowns in communication. These are outlined below.

3.2.1.1 Confirmation check

A confirmation check is used to ensure that the speaker has correctly understood what the previous speaker said. It can be realized by repeating or paraphrasing what the previous speaker said with a rising intonation. For example, see the repetition of *Ten o'clock* in the NS–NNS conversation in text **3j** above.

3.2.1.2 Clarification request

Another important device is the clarification request, which is used when the speaker needs help in understanding what the previous speaker has said. A very common way of asking for clarification is 'What do you mean?' For example:

3k

C: *Do you get satisfaction, though?*

B: *Yes. I reckon you get more satisfaction as you go up the scale as well.*

C: (laughs) *What do you mean, the money scale?*

B: *No, the job, the job.*

(Author's data)

Here, C asks for a clarification of the word *scale*, which he interprets as *the money scale*, and B clarifies that he is referring to the job scale.

In the following piece of data the teacher asks students what their dogs do when they are happy:

3l

T: *Pauline.*

S: *He /wæts/ the chair.*

T: *He wags the chair? How does he wag the chair?*

S: *He wets, wets the chair.*

T: *Wets? He makes them all wet?*

S: *Yes.*

T: *Oh!*

(Author's data)

Because the student pronounces the word *wets* as /wæts/, the teacher mishears it as *wags* and asks the pupil to clarify what she means by *wags the chair*. After the pupil clarifies her previous utterance, the teacher paraphrases her answer and asks for confirmation. In other words, the teacher uses both a clarification request and a confirmation check to try and understand what the pupil is saying.

3.2.1.3 Repetition request

Repetition requests are used when the speaker fails to hear or understand what the previous speaker has said and asks for a repetition or a restatement. It can be in the form of repeating part of the previous speaker's utterance with a rising intonation, the aim being to get them to repeat the rest. (For an example, see text **21**, page 35, lines 17–19.)

A repetition request can also be in the form of an explicit request to the other speaker to repeat, by using expressions like 'I beg your pardon' and 'Please say that again'.

3.2.1.4 Decomposition

Decomposition means breaking up the initial question into several questions, making it easier for the other speaker to respond to it. For example:

3m

NS: *When do you go to the uh Santa Monica? . . . You say you go*
        fishing in Santa Monica, right?
NNS: *Yeah.*
NS: *When?*
(Long 1983b:136)

The NS, upon getting no immediate response to the initial question, establishes the topic of talk by making a statement and asking the NNS to confirm it. When the confirmation is given, the topic is established and the NS then moves on to ask the NNS to provide further information.

3.2.1.5 Comprehension check

Comprehension checks are usually realized by 'Right?', 'OK?' or 'Do you understand?' Long (1983b) considers comprehension checks as strategies for avoiding trouble since, according to him, they show an effort on the part of the native speaker to avoid a communication breakdown. However, they are also used by teachers when students show no sign of comprehension. For example:

3n
T: Can you answer my question? Do you use English or Chinese in class?
S: (silence)
T: Do you understand my question?
S: (muttering)
T: Sorry? Sorry?
S: (in Chinese) *Ask the question once again.*
T: Do you do you speak English or Chinese in class? We speak –
S: We speak English.
(Author's data)

When a response is not forthcoming, a comprehension check is an important device for finding out whether this is because the students/NNSs do not know the answer or because they do not even understand the question.

3.2.1.6 Self-repetition

The term 'self-repetition' is used to refer to all instances where the speaker repeats what they have said previously, whether it is an exact repetition or a repetition in which modifications are made. The various types of modification of questions discussed in the previous section can all be subsumed under 'self-repetition'.

3.3 Student involvement and comprehensible input

While modification devices help ESL students or NNSs to obtain comprehensible input, the number of modification devices used is not necessarily indicative of the amount of input that is comprehensible to the student. This is because, as Tsui (1992) points out, interaction is a two-way process. How much of the input is comprehensible depends not only on how much the NS or teacher modifies the input and the interactional structure in order to <u>provide</u> comprehensible input, but more importantly on how much the NNS or student is involved in trying to <u>obtain</u> comprehensible input. The teacher or NS may use a lot of modification devices and yet still fail to make their input comprehensible. For example:

3o

T: *Where is the place where there are a lot of cocoa beans? Does anybody know the place?*

S: (silence)

T: *What is the name of the place? Does anybody know?*

S: (silence)

T: *Anybody? If you know the answer, tell us. Don't don't speak to the table, all right? Don't say the answer to the table, see?*
(A student puts up his hand.)

T: *Yes?*

S: *My name is Hung Chi Man.*

T: *Your name is what?*

S: *Hung Chi Man.*

T: *Good, Hung Chi Man. Could you please listen to me? Listen to me. My question is, what is the name of the place or what is the place where there are a lot of cocoa beans?*

S: *Your name is Miss Brown.*

(Author's data)

The teacher first modifies the initial question by simplifying the structure of the question. Then she decomposes the initial question *into two questions. What is the name of the place? and Does anybody know?* A student finally puts up his hand, but we can see that he did not understand the question at all. The teacher repeats the question and yet there is still no comprehension. It is very likely that the student catches the word *name* and thinks that he has been asked to give his name. And when the question is repeated he hears the words *me, my* and *name* and thinks the teacher wants him to tell her what her name is.

The problem in text **3o** is that the teacher keeps on modifying the input without any indication from the student of the cause of the breakdown in communication. It is not until the student produces a wrong response that the teacher realizes that her question was not understood. Even then, she has no idea why the question was not understood. As we can see from the data, a repetition of the question did not help.

In Long (1983b), among the six modification devices, comprehension check, self-repetition and decomposition are devices that teachers use to try and make their input comprehensible. Whether they actually succeed in making it comprehensible or not is not known, as has already been demonstrated in text **3o**. Confirmation checks, clarification requests and repetition requests are devices that teachers use to understand students' input rather than to make their own input comprehensible. If, however, they are used by the students, then they are highly indicative that the students are engaged in the negotiation of comprehensible input. Take the following piece of data for example:

3p

T: *So I give you mm ten minutes, is that enough?*

S: *No, not enough.*

T: *Not enough? Fifteen, OK? Fifteen minutes for you to talk it over, try to decide –*

S: *Fifty?*

T: *Fifteen. Fifteen minutes.*

(Author's data)

The student's confirmation check shows that he has misheard fifteen as fifty. The teacher's repetition of the time-limit for the task after the confirmation check ensures that the input is comprehensible.

ACTIVITY

Examine the following conversation. What role do the students play in making the input comprehensible?

3q
(The teacher is giving instructions on homework.)
T: *It's twelve questions about the picture and twelve answers. So what you have to do is look at the pictures, write a question about each picture and then answer the question that you have written and underline the verb in each sentence. There are twelve pictures. Number one has already been done for you. You have to make eleven questions and eleven answers only. That is your homework.*
S1: *Do we need to draw a picture?*
T: *Draw what pictures?*
S1: *The –*
T: *No, you don't have to draw the pictures, just write just write the sentences. All right, now, will you take out your green book four?*
S2: *Mrs. Kent, do we need to write number one on the book?*
T: *No, you don't have to write number one, otherwise it will be twelve pairs of sentences, wouldn't it? Eleven pairs.*
S3: *Do we get the green book four?*
T: *Green book four, yes.*
(Tsui 1992: 52–3)

The teacher's lengthy instruction is immediately followed by a clarification request from S1, which indicates that the student is not clear about the bit of instruction telling them to write a question about each picture. The second student's (S2) clarification request indicates that she is not clear about whether it is necessary to write it down in the book. Finally, the third student (S3) goes back to the teacher's instruction after the first clarification and seeks clarification that she has heard the instruction correctly. We can see that the three clarification requests performed by the students are much more likely to help them obtain input that is comprehensible to them than if these clarification requests were performed by the teacher, or if the teacher had just on her own repeated or modified her instructions.

In text **3q** we have an example of students' active involvement in making input comprehensible to them by seeking clarification from the teacher. Another important role that students have is to help the teacher gauge their level of competence so that the input the latter provides will not be too difficult. One way that students do this is by telling the teacher outright that they don't know how to express something in English.

From the above discussion we can see that it is very important not to take the quantity of modification devices used as the sole indicator of the amount of negotiation work and comprehensible input. In fact Tsui (1992), in a close examination of two ESL classrooms, shows that the lesson with a higher percentage of modification devices does not seem to be providing more comprehensible input. It is also very important to differentiate between modification devices used by teachers to try and <u>provide</u> comprehensible input and those used by students to try and <u>obtain</u> comprehensible input. Finally, it is essential that learners be actively involved in the negotiation of comprehensible input in the classroom.

3.4 Turn-allocation and turn-taking

In the previous section we discussed the importance of student involvement in negotiating comprehensible input. In this section we shall look at another aspect of students' involvement in classroom interaction: their turn-taking behaviour and its relation to language learning. Since the classroom is a place where the teacher is the figure of authority who decides who has the right to speak and when, students' turn-taking behaviour is often affected by the teacher's turn-allocation behaviour.

3.4.1 Turn-allocation behaviour

In general, we may say that the teacher allocates speaking turns to students by either specifying who is to take the turn or by throwing it open to the whole class. The former can be done by nominating or by using gestures such as eye gaze and pointing; Allwright and Bailey (1991: 124) refer to this kind of turn-allocation as a 'personal solicit'. The latter, which can be done by simply asking the question and looking round the class or explicitly stating that anybody can answer the question, is referred to as a 'general solicit'.

A common pattern found in classrooms is that the teacher will start off with a general solicit and, when no student volunteers to take the turn, will resort to a personal solicit to sustain the interaction, to keep the brisk pace of the lesson or to move the lesson forward. The purpose of doing this, for most teachers, is to get everybody's attention, since, if they start with a personal solicit, only the student nominated will be attending to the question or instruction.

Sometimes teachers may also use a general solicit upon getting no response from a personal solicit, so as to take the pressure off the nominated student. Or they may use another personal solicit upon failing to get a response to the first personal solicit, in order to take the pressure off the student who failed to produce the answer and to check round to make sure that students are following the lesson. For example:

3r
T: Well, if I did break my leg, I can't stay away from school until my leg is completely better. I have to come to school with this

thing. Who knows what this thing is called? They are not the same. Some of them are like this (draws on the board). *Some of them are like this, with a handle there, a stick-like thing. Pauline?*

S: (silence)

T: *What kind of people use this thing? People who hurt themselves. What do we call that? Elaine?*

S: *Handicap.*

T: *Handicapped people. Yes.*

(Author's data)

Apart from checking students' knowledge, solicits, be they general or personal, have other functions. Firstly, they are often used as a classroom management device; for example, teachers may direct a personal solicit at a student who is not paying attention in class as a means of focusing their attention. Secondly, they are often used by teachers to structure a lesson, to introduce a topic or to move the lesson forward. The following is the· beginning of a grammar lesson in which the teacher wants to revise ʻverbs of action':

3s

T: *Now, tell me, how many kinds of verbs are there?*

Ss: (raise hands)

T: *Yes, Teresa.*

S: *Two.*

T: *Yes. Who can tell me what the two kinds of verbs are?*

Ss: (raise hands)

T: *Angel.*

S: *Verbs of action and verbs of being.*

T: *Right. Now who can tell me three examples of verbs of action?*

Ss: (raise hands)

T: *Maria.*

S: *running, skipping, jumping.*

. . .

T: *Now, what kind of verb have we been using so far?*

Ss: Verbs of action.
T: Right, those are verbs of action.
(Author's data)

As we can see, the first three general solicits introduce the topic, the first being more general and the second more specific. When the students have given a number of examples of verbs of action, the teacher rounds off the topic by asking another general solicit, *what kind of verb have we been using so far?*

3.4.2   Motivations for turn-allocations

Turn-allocation is something that teachers do so often that it becomes almost automatic. Most experienced teachers are aware that they should not be allocating turns to only a few – that they should try and involve every student. However, what teachers think they have done in the classroom may turn out to be quite different from what they have actually done. The following excerpt from a teacher's report of his classroom action research is illuminating:

more often than not I thought that I tried to choose people at random but I suspected . . . that I asked students I knew would be able to give an answer, thus many of the students were not given a fair chance . . . It was apparent to me after watching the first video and monitoring my subsequent lessons that I unconsciously asked the same students questions. After further analysis, it also appeared that they were for the most part those who I knew would know the answer. (Author's data)

Teachers have different motivations for allocating turns to students. Most teachers tend to allocate more turns to students who are active in class and always ready to volunteer answers. By allocating turns to them the teacher is sure of getting an answer. Some teachers tend to allocate turns to students who enthusiastically bid for turns because they do not want to discourage them. Other teachers allocate turns to brighter students, from whom they are sure of getting a correct answer, in order to make themselves feel good about their own teaching and to reassure themselves that learning is taking place. The following is an excerpt from another teacher's report:

On reflection, I think this has a lot to do with the nature of the teacher. As a teacher, I can identify that I have a need to feel successful, a good way to have this reaffirmed is to ask those students who I know will give me the answer that I want – what better way to show that 'real' learning is taking place! If I ask others I may run the risk of finding out that some students haven't understood what I have so painstakingly been teaching. That then means I have to re-evaluate my methods and the responsibility is back on me. (Author's data)

Some teachers allocate turns to students who are likely to know the answer because they want to save time and cover more material. Some do so because they want to avoid silence and embarrassment. The following excerpt from the reflection of a teacher is likely to be shared by many teachers:

I often ask them [students who put up their hands] to answer questions because I want to save time. Normally they would not put up their hands if they do not know the answer. Then I do not need to explain the answer and can cover more in the lesson ... I am afraid of silence in class. Sometimes when I ask a student a question and he does not know the answer, he will just stand up and keep quiet. When I ask another student to help him, this student may also keep quiet because he does not know the answer as well. But if I ask the one who puts up his hand, there will not be a moment of silence. (Author's data)

While it is impossible to allocate turns evenly in every single lesson, an uneven allocation of turns for a long period of time will make the weak and shy students feel neglected. The more they feel neglected, the more reluctant they will be to participate.

It is also important to remember that different tasks may require different turn-allocation behaviours. For example, if the teacher is asking recall questions, which check if students have got the facts right, then the teacher may go round the class, giving everybody a chance to provide short answers. If the teacher is asking thinking questions, he or she may want to ask bright students, who are likely to provide interesting answers, in order to start a lively discussion.

3.4.3 Turn-taking behaviour

Generally speaking, students' turn-taking behaviour can be divided into solicited turns and unsolicited turns. An example of the former is a turn taken when a teacher seeks an answer to a question; students may answer the question when they are specifically nominated to do so or they may take the initiative to answer it (this is often referred to as a 'self-selected' turn). An unsolicited (or 'initiating') turn is one in which a student initiates a contribution. Initiating turns are always 'self-selected'.

A turn-taking behaviour that many teachers are either not aware of or attach little importance to is 'private' turns taken by students. Allwright (1980), in a pilot study of the turn-taking behaviour of learners, found that one of the learners, who was considered indifferent and uninterested in the language lesson by the teacher, in fact took many quiet, private turns, which were unnoticed. He practised the target language through talk directed at himself and not shared with the teacher or other learners. In another study, in one fifteen-minute segment of a lesson, a teacher directed twenty questions at the students, of which ten were responded to by private turns. If these private turns went unnoticed by the teacher, the level of participation would be very low and the students would not have as many opportunities to practise the target language. Therefore, it is very important for teachers to look out for students taking private turns and, if it is agreeable to the student, to get him or her to make their turn public. The sensitivity of the teacher towards students' turn-taking behaviour is particularly important in classrooms where the students are shy and apprehensive about contributing in class.

3.4.4 Turn-taking behaviour and language learning

In 3.4.1 we saw that teachers' turn-allocation is inextricably linked with students' turn-taking behaviour. Students who are ready to take turns inevitably get more turns allocated to them and hence get more opportunities to practise the target language.

Seliger (1977) studied the participation of adult ESL learners in the classroom and its relation to their language achievement. He proposed that there are two types of language learners, one which he referred to as high-input generators (HIGs) and the other as low-input generators (LIGs). The former are those who, by actively participating in conversations, cause other people to provide them with language input. The latter are those who participate minimally and hence deprive themselves of the opportunity to get input from other people. Seliger observed the classroom behaviour of six learners, three LIGs and three HIGs, and studied their perform-ance in two English tests; he also investigated their use of English outside the classroom. He found that HIGs achieve higher scores in tests and also have more contact with the language outside of class, with native speakers of English. He concluded that students who initiate interactions are better language learners (see Seliger 1983).

While Seliger's conclusion appeals to our intuition as teachers about the relation between active participation in class and progress in learning, this relation is by no means firmly established, and other studies have produced different results.

3.4.5 Turn-taking behaviour and cultural factors

Apart from teachers' turn-allocation, students' turn-taking behav-iour is also intertwined with their cultural background. Research on classroom behaviour of ethnic minorities has shown that there are different cultural expectations of what is considered permissible in the classroom. Sato (1982) studied the turn-taking behaviours of

Asian and non-Asian students. She found that the former, which includes Japanese, Korean and Chinese, as a group took significantly fewer 'self-selected' turns than the latter. Duff (1986) studied the interaction between Chinese and Japanese learners and found that there was a significant tendency for the Chinese subjects to dominate the interaction. In other words, when looking at students' turn-taking behaviour in the classroom, it is important for teachers to take into consideration the cultural backgrounds of the students, when they are interacting with the teacher and when they are interacting with each other. (See also chapter 4 for a discussion of cultural factors and participation in class.)

PROJECTS

1. In the following piece of classroom data the teacher is using a newspaper article for reading comprehension. The title of the article is 'Police to pursue crooked cabbies'. The teacher asks the students to look at the title and respond to her question 'What are involved?' Examine the following piece of data. Why does the teacher fail to get any response from the students? How would you modify questions to help students to provide a response?

3t

T: *Anyone can tell me now?*

Ss: (silence – 5.27 seconds)

T: *No? What are involved? Well, police to pursue crooked cabbies.*

Ss: (silence – 5.05 seconds)

T: *What are involved? You read this title. You know what cabbies are?*

Ss: (silence – 2.04 seconds; some students nod their heads)

T: *Yeah? You know what police are?*

Ss: (silence – 3.45 seconds; some students nod their heads)

T: *Yes? So we see there is, police is involved and cabbies are involved. Right?*

(Author's data)

2. Video- or audio-record your own lesson. View or listen to the recording. Firstly, examine the questions for which you failed to obtain student responses and identify the possible causes of difficulties. Modify them to make them easier for students to respond to. Secondly, examine the modification devices used, if any, and see whether they were effective in bringing about comprehensible input.

SUMMARY

- The provision of comprehensible input is essential in order for learning to take place.
- Since a very high proportion of teacher talk is taken up by teacher questions, the modification of teacher questions to make them comprehensible to learners is very important.
- The interactional structure between the teacher and the learners must be modified in order for comprehensible input to be negotiated.
- The involvement of students in the negotiation of input is crucial in determining whether input has been made comprehensible or not.
- The turn-taking behaviour of students may be affected by cultural factors, and teachers should be sensitive to students' cultural backgrounds.

4   Student talk

In the discussion so far we have been emphasizing the importance of student involvement in classroom learning. An important form of involvement is students' participation in classroom interaction. However, this is precisely the problem that most teachers face: getting students to respond to their questions, raise questions, offer ideas and make comments. Studies conducted on classroom interaction have shown that student talk accounts for an average of less than 30 per cent of talk in teacher-fronted classrooms. Yet studies on language and learning have shown that children not only learn to talk but they also talk to learn. This can be seen from the fact that children are persistent questioners; it is by asking questions that they explore and learn about the world around them. However, studies have shown that the number of questions asked by children drops significantly as soon as they enter school.

Although one should avoid making the sweeping generalization that there is a simple equation between talking and learning, and should not force students to participate when they are not ready, one cannot deny that participation is very important in language learning. This is because, when students respond to the teacher's or their fellow students' questions, raise queries and give comments, they are actively involved in the negotiation of comprehensible input, which is essential to language acquisition. And when students produce the target language and try to make themselves understood, they are in fact testing out the hypotheses they are forming about the language. Swain (1985) points out that the production of comprehensible output is also essential to the acquisition of the target language.

4.1   Student participation in ESL classrooms

The problem of student participation is even more acute in ESL classrooms. It is not only difficult to get students to initiate questions and volunteer answers, but also to get them to respond to teacher questions even when they are called upon to do so. In Tsui's study (forthcoming), thirty-eight ESL teachers who were enrolled on an in-service training course were asked to identify a problem on which they wished to conduct classroom action research, and over 70 per cent identified getting student oral response as one of their major problems. The following are extracts from some of the teachers' reports:

During English lessons, there was a general lack of response to questions asked. Students were eager to learn and yet they seemed unable to bring themselves to participate actively in class.

. . . the pupils [students] were very passive and quiet. Even when they were called on to ask questions and comment, they kept silent.

Very often my questions were met with silence. And I had to nominate or even force a student to answer or perform a task.

4.2   Contributing factors in student reticence

In Tsui's study (forthcoming) the following factors were identified by teachers as contributing to students' reluctance to speak up in class.

Firstly, most teachers thought that low English proficiency is an important factor. They reported that most of the time it was not so much that students did not know the answer but that they did not know how to express it in English.

ACTIVITY

Consider the following piece of classroom data in the light of the low English proficiency factor. How do we explain the student's behaviour?

4a

T: And what does speaking for the motion mean? Is there anyone who wants to answer this question?

Ss: (no response)

T: OK, Natalie, when I say you are speaking <u>for</u> the motion, what do I mean?

N: Um . . . you mean I . . . I support the motion.

T: Correct. Very good. Thank you for your attention.

(Tsui forthcoming)

The above piece of data shows that the student, Natalie, does know the answer and can express it in English. However, she did not provide the answer until she was specifically nominated by the teacher to do so. It is very likely that Natalie was not the only student who knew the answer but withheld it. This means that there are other factors contributing to students' reluctance to participate actively.

Many teachers in Tsui's study reported that their students were afraid of making mistakes and being laughed at by their peers. The following are some of the teachers' reports:

They are unwilling to speak in English for fear that they may make silly mistakes in front of the brighter students.

Sometimes, students are inactive because they are weak in English and cannot express themselves in English. But some students are inactive simply because they are shy or afraid of making mistakes.

(Tsui forthcoming)

One of the teachers actually asked the students individually why they were so quiet when she asked them questions and whether they prepared their lessons or not. She found out that in fact most of them did prepare for the lesson but 'they were afraid of losing face in front of their classmates if they gave [me] the wrong answer.'

Walker (ongoing), in a piece of research on foreign-language learning anxiety, interviewed a S6 (Grade 12) student, Bob, who was very quiet in class. The following is an excerpt from the interview:

Interviewer: Bob, OK, so you're quiet because you don't know what the teacher's saying.

Bob: Also I have not self-confidence.

Interviewer: Uhuh. Why is that?

Bob: I think my English is not quite good. . . . Sometimes I really frighten, but if I know . . . understand the question, I will answer with self-confidence.

Interviewer: I see. What if you don't understand the question? Do you ask the teacher what he means? Or don't you ask a question?

Bob: Sometimes.

Interviewer: . . . Why don't you ask the question every time you don't understand? Why?

Bob: Why? . . . Sometimes I think I will . . . I think my teacher don't like me.

Interviewer: Why?

Bob: I'm afraid my classmate will laugh. . . . I think my English level is not good, so I am shy to talk English . . .

We can see from the above interview that another important factor is students' lack of confidence in their language proficiency and the fear of making mistakes and being laughed at. The pressure to give the right answer is present in every classroom (see Morgan and Saxton 1991). In the language classroom the pressure is exacerbated by the fact that not only do students have to know the right answer but they also have to express it in the target language. And when they feel that their English is not good enough they prefer to remain silent rather than run the risk of making mistakes. Sometimes this kind of pressure is self-imposed, but it is often also teacher-induced. A teacher in Tsui's study reported as follows: 'Though my attitude might be gentle and encouraging, I was expecting some correct answer most of the time. Given the [sensitive] nature of class, they would feel the strain and were less willing to contribute unless they felt that they have got the "right answer".'

The intolerance of silence was another factor identified by some of the teachers in Tsui's study. This results in very short wait-times after a question has been asked and is a widespread phenomenon. Here is an example:

4b

(The teacher is teaching a passage on drug abuse and going over the reading comprehension questions with the students.)

T: ... *Can you look at the pie chart on page 59? Can you tell me, according to the chart, how many drug addicts are there in Hong Kong? How many? How many?*

S: *Forty – fourteen.*

T: *Can you read the figure? Forty thousand, forty thousand! Ah, how many of them are under thirty, under thirty? About how many? About –* (looking at the students) *twenty thousand! You think this is a lot? Do you think it is quite serious? Think for yourself. Quick. Do you have any friends or relatives who have taken drugs or have tried taking drugs before? Think ...*

The teacher asks one question after another without giving students very much time to come up with an answer. In addition, she chases the students up by telling them to give an answer quickly. Most teachers do not realize that they behave more or less the same way as the teacher above, and are often surprised by the short wait-time they give to students when they listen to the recordings of their own lessons.

In Tsui's study some teachers, after listening to or watching the recordings of their own lessons, reflected on why they were so intolerant of silence:

I do not pause that much because I am afraid that students chat during lessons, they become noisy. Besides, I have the idea that pausing is equal to silence ... Furthermore, time is precious, too precious ...

... to me, silence is a result of [the] teacher's inertia; when silence occurs, it means [the] teacher is not making the lesson productive enough for students to learn . . .

. . . silence gives me the sense of failure because in my hidden vision success means being quick and highly efficient . . . I speak a lot because deep down I believe that teaching, effective teaching, is imparting knowledge all the time . . . Consequently, I hiddenly feel that I would not do my duty and would be a failure unless I spoke a lot.
(Tsui forthcoming)

From the teachers' reflections we can see that one reason is the pressure to get through the curriculum and another is to stop students from chatting and getting noisy. As White and Lightbown (1984) point out, teachers are afraid that a longer wait-time will slow down the pace of the lesson and lead to boredom and disruption in the classroom. Another reason has to do with the teacher's belief about his or her role as a teacher. As can be seen from two of the teachers' reflections above, silence to them is a sign of their own incompetence and inadequacy in fulfilling their role as an imparter of knowledge.

Another important factor in student reticence that some of the teachers identified was the teacher's subconscious choice to allocate speaking turns to brighter students. As pointed out in section 3.4.2, the uneven allocation could be in order to save time so that more can be covered in a lesson, since brighter students are more likely to provide the right answer and therefore less time will be 'wasted' in waiting for the answer, in guiding the student towards the right answer, or in explaining why their answer is wrong. The uneven allocation could also be due to the teacher's ego, as one teacher reflected in Tsui's study (see p. 76, extract beginning 'On reflection . . .'). The consequence of this is that weaker students will feel ignored, their confidence will be further undermined and they could become even more reluctant to participate.

A final factor identified by the teachers was incomprehensible input. Teachers reported that their students found their questions difficult to understand. However, since the students did not indicate this to the teacher, no repair was done and this led to further incomprehension and hence further silence.

4.3 Language learning anxiety

In the above discussion we can see that much of students' reluctance to participate in classroom interaction has to do with apprehension, fear, nervousness and worry. This is hardly surprising since the classroom is a place where there is an unequal power relationship between the teacher and the students; this is bound to generate anxiety.

Classroom anxiety is a phenomenon that is found in all classrooms. However, the anxiety generated by second-language learning is unique. In learning a language, the student has to master the target language and perform in that language at the same time. This is a very unsettling process since they have to perform in a language that they know they are not competent in and perhaps are struggling very hard to master. This will inevitably make students feel that they are unable to represent themselves fully. This has a tremendous impact on students' self-perception and self-confidence. The anxiety is further exacerbated by the fact that in the language classroom the teacher often focuses not only on the correctness of student performance in terms of content but also in terms of form. In section 2.3.5 we saw how teachers can sometimes be very persistent in getting students to produce answers that are correct in both form and content, perhaps without realizing that by doing this they could be publicly humiliating the student.

4.4 Studies of foreign-language classroom anxiety

Research on anxiety makes a distinction between 'trait anxiety' and 'state anxiety'. The former refers to a personality characteristic, for example a person who is generally nervous and tense, whereas the latter refers to anxiety that is specific to a situation, for example stage fright. Foreign-language classroom anxiety is a kind of state anxiety that is specific to the foreign-language classroom. A distinction is also made between 'facilitating anxiety' and 'debilitating anxiety' (Kleinmann 1977, Scovel 1978). The former refers to the kind of anxiety that helps a person to try harder and consequently perform better. The latter refers to the kind of anxiety that hinders good performance, and it is this kind of anxiety that is under discussion here.

Various studies have been done on the effects of debilitating anxiety on second- or foreign-language learning. For example, Kleinmann (1977) found that different types of grammatical constructions were attempted by highly anxious students and less anxious students. Steinberg and Horwitz (1986) found that learners attempt more concrete, less interpretative messages when they are in an anxiety-producing situation than when they are in a more relaxed situation.

Based on three related performance anxieties – communication apprehension, test anxiety and fear of negative evaluation – and discussions with two groups of fifteen students, Horwitz, Horwitz and Cope (1991) developed a Foreign Language Classroom Anxiety Scale to identify students who are highly anxious. It was administered to seventy-five university students studying introductory Spanish at the University of Texas. They found that nearly half of the students reported that they started to panic when they had to speak without preparation in their language classes, one-third reported that they got nervous and confused when they were speaking in their language classes, over one-quarter reported that they felt very self-conscious when they had to speak the foreign language in front of other students, and slightly under half the students rejected the statement that they felt confident when they spoke in foreign-language classes.

Studies such as Horwitz's show that language learning anxiety is a distinctly identifiable anxiety, which has adverse effects on language learning. The factors that teachers identified as contributing to students' reluctance to participate in class are precisely those elements that underlie this anxiety. Students with low English proficiency are bound to feel that their self-esteem is being undermined when they are required to speak in front of their peers. The avoidance of participation is an attempt to protect one's self-image by avoiding the risk of making a mistake, being laughed at by peers, and being negatively evaluated by the teacher. And, as Tsui (forthcoming) points out, it is important that language teachers recognize that 'beneath their apparent apathy in the ESL classroom, anxious students are desperately trying to avoid humiliation, embarrassment and criticisms, and to preserve self-esteem . . . They [teachers] must appreciate the extent to which students' behaviour can be affected by it and the extent to which teachers' behaviour can exacerbate it. Otherwise, whatever strategies the teacher adopts to overcome the problem are doomed to failure.' Indeed, in Tsui's study it was found that successful strategies used by teachers to address the problem of students' reticence were those that minimize language learning anxiety – for example, establishing a good relationship with students, allowing students to discuss with their peers before offering answers, and using group work. The unsuccessful strategies were those that exacerbate anxiety, for example trying to get a student to answer a question when he or she is not ready to do so.

4.5 Cultural factors in student participation

In discussing student participation Allwright and Bailey (1991) cautioned that students should not be forced to participate before they are ready to do so; they were referring to the teacher's sensitivity to the learning style of individual students. Another aspect that teachers need to be sensitive to is the cultural background of learners. Allwright and Bailey point out that some learners who are very competent in the target language and who know that they are better than their peers may be reluctant to participate in class because they do not want to stand out from the rest of the class, and yet they do not want to make the same mistakes as their peers for fear of criticism by the teacher. This phenomenon is prevalent among Chinese students, whose culture emphasizes modesty. A study conducted by Wong in 1984 (cited in Wu 1993: 62) on the sociocultural factors affecting students' classroom behaviour found that there are certain rules that Chinese students in Hong Kong abide by:

— You should not demonstrate verbal success in English in front of your peers.
— You should hesitate and show difficulty in arriving at an answer.
— You should not answer the teacher voluntarily or enthusiastically in English.
— You should not speak fluent English.

4.6 Small group talk

In view of the language learning anxiety that students suffer in the classroom, it is important that as language teachers we try to create a relaxing atmosphere, in which students feel comfortable to try out the target language and make mistakes. One effective way of doing this is by using group work. The value of small group work is well documented. It has been widely observed that students are much more ready to interact with each other than with their teachers. The responses that they produce when interacting with peers also tend to be more complex than when they are interacting with teachers. In the rest of this section we shall examine the kind of student talk that small group work is likely to generate and why.

4.6.1 Quantity of talk

Compared with lockstep teaching, group work provides more opportunities for learners to practise the target language. This is hardly surprising since in a teacher-fronted classroom teacher talk takes up on average more than two-thirds of classroom talk (Flanders 1970). Long and Porter (1985) observe that in a fifty-minute lesson of a class of thirty students in a public secondary school classroom, the opportunity to speak for each student is thirty seconds per lesson or one hour per year. They point out that the lack of opportunity to practise the target language, especially the oral-aural skills, is one of the main reasons for the low achievement of many classroom second-language learners.

Apart from simple arithmetic, a very important reason for there being more student talk in group work is the removal of the figure of authority, that is, the teacher. When students work with their peers, their contributions will not be evaluated as right or wrong because there is nobody who has the authority to do so.

4.6.2 Exploratory talk

The removal of authority in small group work changes the mode of interaction from an evaluative mode to a sharing mode. This encourages students to take risks in the sense that they will verbalize their ideas even when these are not fully developed and coherent and they will use the target language even when they are not sure whether it is grammatically right or wrong. Barnes (1976) refers to this kind of talk as 'exploratory talk' as opposed to 'final draft talk', in which whatever is expressed is a final product presented for evaluation. Barnes points out that while teacher-fronted class-rooms typically generate 'final draft talk', small group work typi-cally generates 'exploratory talk'. The characteristics of exploratory talk are a more tentative and less definitive language use, more vagueness, more false starts, that is, changing direction in the middle of an utterance, more hesitations and stuttering.

The following excerpt is taken from a group discussion by four students in an S7 (Grade 13) ESL class where students were given the task of talking about the 'Big Sister Scheme' that their school was going to organize in order to tackle the problem of student suicide, which was becoming more and more serious.

4c

(The students have started the discussion and have been talking about students feeling upset when they have poor examination results.)

1 *S1:* ... *And if it is not enough for them to solve their unfavourable*
2 *results problem =*
3 *S2: Mhm*
4 *S1: = um they can go for help from their teachers to discuss with*
5 *their friends. And also we we we is it possible for us to organize*
6 *a um a reading reading campaign to them? Mainly um we can*
7 *group among them after school so that they can improve ah or*
8 *ah to exchange their their ah their study skill or technique to*
9 *each other so that they can gain more and also improve their*
10 *study skill.*
11 *S2: Mm, that's a good idea. Um so*
12 *S1: What do you think, Joey?*
13 *S3: Um Um s s ah, I think commit suicide is ah coming from large*
14 *(inaudible) families problem. And I think we should ah better ah*
15 *in is ah we invited their family members like mother father to*
16 *school and give them some plays around school. And from this*
17 *play they can realize their their daughters' thinking and and*
18 *problems like ah all right ah some games ah*
19 *S1: Do you think some games that parents and students should play*
20 *together and also –*
21 *S3: Play together.*
22 *S1: Play together. Do you mean that so that they can communicate.*
23 *Ah they can know more to each other. I think it*
24 *S4: Ah is it possible for us to make a series and then show it*
25 *to students?*
25 [
26 *S2: Make make what?*
27 *S4: A programme.*
28 *S2: Make a programme.*

29 *S1:   What programme do you think?*
30 *S4:   Ah informal, to encourage them to talk talk more to parents and*
31 *   teachers and in some cases* (pause)
32 *S1:   Maybe um connection with ah between parents and stu and their*
33 *   child and also student and teachers is very important.*
                        [
34 *S2:   Mhm.*
(Lee 1993a)

As we can see from the above excerpt, there are many instances of
hesitations like *um* and *ah*, as well as stuttering. Vague expressions
are used, for example *so that they can gain more* (line 9), where the
object of *gain* is not specified. Tentative expressions like *is it
possible* (line 24) and *maybe* (line 32) are also found. All of these
are typically used when the speaker is thinking aloud and are not
frequently found in teacher-fronted classrooms, where students'
contributions are evaluated by the teacher. We can also see that
there are instances of changing direction in the middle of an
utterance (lines 5, 14–15) and stopping in the middle of an utterance
(line 31). These are typical of exploratory talk, where speakers do
not have to have fully developed ideas in mind before they start
speaking.

4.6.3   Nature of interaction

Removing the figure of authority and putting students in small
groups not only creates a more permissive atmosphere and increases
the quantity of talk, it fundamentally changes the nature of the
interaction. In teacher-fronted classrooms the teacher nominates
topics, allocates turns, monitors the direction of talk and structures
the discussion. In small groups students have to take on the
responsibility of managing talk and determining the direction of
the discussion themselves. In fact, when no discussion leader is
appointed, one group member usually takes on that role. In text **4c**

above, although no group leader was appointed, S1 took on the role of leader by starting off the discussion with *As our school is a girls' college, maybe the students would concern about the relationship between boys and girls, so that we would ah take more act on concerning their their thinking about the relationship between ah their opposite sex* . . . She tried to involve quiet members of the group in the discussion, for example, *What do you think, Joey?* (line 12). She also tried to carry the discussion forward by asking or helping members to elaborate on their suggestion. For example, she helped S3 to develop the idea of introducing games between parents and students (lines 19–23) and she asked and helped S4 to elaborate on her suggestion to make a programme for students (lines 28, 32–33). It was also S1 who concluded the discussion by saying, *So we can conclude that for us we will be concern more concern more um with how to improve their Ah their problem* . . .

ACTIVITY

Examine the following excerpt from a group discussion. Who would you say has taken on the role of leading the discussion?

4d

The students were given the task of deciding what they would do in an anti-smoking campaign.

B: So, firstly, I guess we should decide what form should . . . uh . . . this . . . this . . . thing should be . . . So, should it be . . . eh exhibition, ah . . . debate, or and, ah . . .

C: I give my support on exhibition.

A: Me too.

B: Yes.

D: I think it will be better than an essay.

B: Yes. But I think it's better be in a debate form.

A: Why is debate?

B: Because if we take this in a debate form we can understand the

.. the ... the supporting the supporting ... points more clearly and in exhibition we can only see the positive things about cigarette smoking and not ... ah ... not the ... the ... not the ... side ... not the negative sides of this ...

C: About the ... your your opinion will be very limited to only one group of people. But exhibition can open to the ... to all walks of the society ... And it will be an advantage and can benefit to more people.

B: Yeah, but a debate can be held many times also so I guess we can we can also.

C: But not many people ... will ... ah ... pay their interest in ... the ... the debate form.

B: So –

A: She say my things.

D: I think exhibition would be better.

B: OK ... exhibition ... then ... ah ... what should be inside exhibition?

(Fullilove 1992)

In the above excerpt B and C are the more vocal ones and they each put forward their proposals. However, B is the one who takes on the role of discussion leader. B starts the discussion going by taking the floor first and suggesting that the group should initially decide on the form. And when the majority of the group members support an exhibition, he moves the topic forward to discuss the content of the exhibition (see the last line in the excerpt above). Although B leads the discussion, his role is different from that of a teacher. He does not have the final word on the decisions. The students collaborate in arriving at a decision as to which is the best form of publicity for an anti-smoking campaign. This example as well as text **4c** illustrates how conducive group work is in getting students to take on the responsibility of managing talk. It is not meant to suggest that there is no need to appoint a group leader in group discussions.

4.6.4 Variety of speech functions

Group work provides the opportunity to practise a much wider range of speech functions. In lockstep teaching the predominant pattern of interaction is the teacher asking display questions rather than referential questions, students answering questions to display knowledge, and the teacher giving feedback on the answer. There is little opportunity for students to perform other speech functions that are frequently found in genuine communication, for example requesting and accepting/declining requests, challenging other people's point of view, and so on. As a result, students have little opportunity to develop the kind of conversational skill that is needed outside the classroom. Group work enables students to engage in genuine communication, where the message is more important than the form. As Long and Porter (1985) point out, group work enables learners to develop discourse competence rather than just linguistic competence at the sentence level.

ACTIVITY

Consider text **4d** again and analyse the extract in terms of the language functions performed by the students. Would you find students performing these language functions in a teacher-fronted classroom?

Language Function:

Proposing, asking for suggestions	B:	*So, firstly, I guess we should decide what form should . . . uh . . . this . . . this . . . thing should be . . . So, should it be . . . eh exhibition, ah . . . debate, or and, ah . . .*
Making a suggestion	C:	*I give my support on exhibition.*
Supporting the suggestion	A:	*Me too.*
Acknowledging	B:	*Yes.*
Supporting and giving reasons	D:	*I think it will be better than an essay.*

96

Making alternative suggestions	B: Yes. But I think it's better be in a debate form.
Requesting explanation	A: Why is debate?
Explaining	B: Because if we take this in a debate form we can understand the . . . the . . . the supporting the supporting . . . points more clearly and in exhibition we can only see the positive things about cigarette smoking and not . . . ah . . . not the . . . the . . . not the . . . side . . . not the negative sides of this . . .
Disagreeing	C: About the . . . your your opinion will be very limited to only one group of people. But exhibition can open to the . . . to all walks of the society . . . And it will be an advantage and can benefit to more people.
Disagreeing	B: Yeah, but a debate can be held many times also so I guess we can we can also.
Disagreeing	C: But not many people . . . will . . . ah . . . pay their interest in . . . the . . . the debate form.
	B: So –
Agreeing (with C)	A: She say my things.
Supporting (C)	D: I think exhibition would be better.
Conceding, asking for suggestions	B: OK . . . exhibition . . . then . . . ah . . . what should be inside exhibition?

As we can see from the above analysis, students performed a large variety of language functions, for example asking for suggestions, agreeing and disagreeing with each other, proposing and conceding, most of which are absent in a teacher-fronted classroom dominated by teacher question–student response–teacher feedback interaction.

4.6.5 Collaborative construction of meaning

In teacher-fronted classrooms, when students are lost for words they naturally turn to the teacher rather than their peers for help. Very often the teacher's words are the verdict. In small group talk, because of the absence of the teacher, students sometimes help each other out when they are lost for words. The following is a continuation of text **4d**:

4e
B: *OK ... Exhibition ... Then ... ah ... what should be inside exhibition?*
A: *Ah. What information can we get? Can we get the economic of the smokers and their relevance and the expenditure?*
C: *Statistic.*
A: *No, chee ... The smokers' expenditure and the relevance ... their*
B: *Relationships.*
A: *Relationships, yes.*
(Fullilove 1992)

In the last three lines A is trying to find the word 'relationship' and B steps in to help. Here we have an utterance that is collaboratively constructed by two people.

4.6.6 Negotiation of comprehensible input

Varonis and Gass (1985) studied the interaction of NNSs with each other as opposed to NSs and found that, when NNSs are involved in genuine communication with each other, there is more negotiation for message meaning. Doughty and Pica (1986) compared the difference in the number of 'conversational adjustments' found in group work, pair work and lockstep teaching – the adjustments including comprehension checks, confirmation requests, clarification requests, self- and other repetitions, as well as repairs.

They found that more negotiation work is found in group work and pair work than in lockstep teaching.

The negotiation of comprehensible input in group work can be seen from the following piece of data.

4f

B: *Yes, or someone . . . some . . . more practical thing can be done in the exhibition.*

A: *What practical?*

B: *Like . . .? Some . . . ah . . .*

A: *Experiment.*

B: *Yeah, experiment.*

(Fullilove 1992)

B's suggestion of putting *some more practical thing* in the exhibition is followed up by A, who asks him to clarify what he means. In response B tries to think of an example and is helped out by A, who supplies the word *experiment*, which is accepted by A as what he means.

In the above discussion we have outlined the features of small group talk and how this kind of talk is conducive to students acquiring the target language. Despite the many advantages of group work, both from educational and language acquisition points of view, there are still teachers who are reluctant to introduce group work in their own classrooms. One of the reasons commonly put forward by teachers is that group work is very noisy and difficult to monitor. This could well be due to the fear among teachers that, if their classrooms are full of talk, they will be viewed as incompetent since their class appears to be out of control (Morgan and Saxton 1991). Undoubtedly, group work is more difficult to manage than lockstep teaching. It needs to be well planned, structured and interesting before students will be fully engaged and will benefit from it. But the studies on group work so far have shown that the effort is worthwhile. The advantage of small group talk is best summarized by a quotation from Dillon (1988: 154):

A changed environment is a learning motivator: it presents opportunities for those students whose learning styles do not fit the traditional classroom model; it changes the position and the status of the teacher, enabling changes in class empowerment; it promotes a different kind of talk and opportunities for peer learning and teaching. Students more readily engage in question and answer exchanges with each other than their teachers and students' responses to fellow students are longer and more complex than responses to the teacher.

PROJECT

Make a comparison between a lockstep discussion and a small group discussion. If you have a class of thirty, split them into two groups. With one group, conduct a lockstep discussion, preferably on a problem-solving task, and record and transcribe the discussion. With the other group, divide them into groups of four or five and ask them to discuss the same task; record and transcribe their discussions. Compare the two types of discussion according to the following dimensions:

—who takes on the role of managing the discussion;
—quantity of talk – in terms of the number and the length of turns taken by students;
—quality of talk – in terms of the number of instances where students use clarification requests, confirmation checks, repetition requests, self-correction, other-correction, collaborative construction of meaning;
—variety of speech functions used by students.

SUMMARY

- Students' reticence to participate in class is related to the phenomenon of language learning anxiety, which has been little attended to in language learning research until recently.
- It is important that as language teachers we understand and appreciate the psychological experience that learners are going

through and try to alleviate their anxiety. One effective means of doing so is to introduce group work where the figure of authority is removed, hence removing the evaluative mode of interaction and the threatening nature of 'performing' in front of a large audience.

- The collaborative nature of small group work is conducive to students sharing ideas that may not be fully formed, and helping each other to clarify and construct meaning.
- The group work setting enables students to be involved in more natural conversation, in which they have the opportunity to use a variety of speech functions and hence to develop their discourse competence, not just linguistic competence.

5 Classroom observation

In the previous four chapters we have discussed various aspects of
classroom interaction and illustrated the discussion with excerpts
from a number of lessons. However, so far we have not looked at a
lesson in its entirety and tried to describe what actually went on in
that particular lesson, nor have we made a systematic analysis of a
particular aspect of classroom interaction in a lesson. This is
necessary and worthwhile because teachers are often so involved in
the lesson itself that what they think they are doing is often quite
different from what they are actually doing. Teachers who record
and analyse their own lessons for the first time almost always
report that they find the experience embarrassing and revealing.

In making descriptions of classroom interaction, the inevitable
questions that need to be answered are: What are the criteria for
the descriptive statements made? Will different people examining
the same piece of classroom data come up with similar descriptions?
To answer these questions we need descriptive systems or observation instruments that are replicable.

Earlier classroom studies relied heavily on the use of observational instruments with predetermined categories in coding classroom data. More recent studies advocate an ethnographic approach, in which the observer examines the data in its entire
context with no preconceived ideas and tries to understand what
goes on in the classroom from the perspective of participants. In
this chapter we shall look very briefly at some of the influential
observational instruments, what purpose they serve, and some of
the criticisms of this approach to classroom observation. We shall
then outline an alternative approach to classroom observation:
ethnographic observation.

5.1 Systematic classroom observation

The term 'systematic observation' has been defined by McIntyre and Macleod as follows:

> By systematic observation procedures, we mean those procedures in which the observer, deliberately refraining from participation in classroom activities, analyses aspects of these activities through the use of a predetermined set of categories or signs. This analysis may take place during the observation, or may be based on selective records such as audio and video recordings, or on transcripts of classroom discourse. (1986:10)

Systematic observation of language classrooms started in the sixties with the aim of distinguishing and monitoring the effectiveness of different methods in foreign-language teaching. Observation schedules were developed to describe what went on in the classroom in order to ensure that the prescribed teaching methods were followed and that the learning outcomes were the result of the application of a certain method. The inconclusive findings, however, led researchers to question whether there is indeed a superior method. At the same time, other needs for systematic observation arose: the need for teacher educators to make an objective evaluation of and feedback on teaching as well as the need to describe actual classroom behaviour regardless of the method used. One of the earliest observation systems was Moskowitz's Foreign Language Interaction (FLint) (1967), an adaptation of Flanders's Interaction Analysis Categories (FIAC) (1970).

5.2 Limitations of systematic observation

Systematic observation as an approach to classroom studies has been criticized for merely focusing on quantitative data analysis, hence overlooking important information that can only be obtained by qualitative data analysis. It has also been criticized for using predetermined categories, a fundamental characteristic of all systematic observation procedures. The drawbacks of using predetermined categories are, firstly, that the coder or viewer's analysis of data is constrained by the categories, and it is easy for them to consider information which may be crucial to the lesson as irrelevant; this prevents the teacher or researcher from gaining a full understanding of the complexities in classroom processes. Secondly, in trying to map the categories on to the data, the coder often tends to force the data into the categories, hence giving a distorted picture of the classroom.

A third limitation of systematic observation is that, by using a checklist of coding schemes during observations, data are treated as isolated, discrete entities, which bear no relationship with each other. This 'obscures the sequential flow of classroom activities' (Mehan 1979:12). Such isolated units based on time also fail to show the context in which they occur. This is a serious drawback because, as Mehan further points out, 'The relationship of an action to ... context is important, for actions take on different meanings in different phases of an event, in different events, and at different times of the year' (1979:13).

A fourth limitation is that the coder, as an outsider, may not be able to understand or may misinterpret the talk between the teacher and the students, and among the students themselves, since he or she does not have access to their shared meanings, which are generated by the cultural and historical context of that particular classroom. A fifth limitation is that this kind of description does not take into account the meanings that participants give to their interaction. Delamont and Hamilton (1976) point out that systematic observation focuses on what is observable, that is, what the teacher and the students do, and misses out on what is not observable, that is, the mental activities behind these actions, such as their perceptions of their own or other participants' actions.

In the following section we shall examine an alternative descriptive system.

5.3 An alternative descriptive system – FOCUS

Unlike interaction action analysis, Fanselow (1977) emphasizes the importance of the setting in which the communication occurs and the contextual details. In FOCUS (Foci for Observing Communications Used in Settings), five dimensions of communication are taken into consideration: source, pedagogical purpose, medium, use and content. This system, according to Fanselow, enables us to give a comprehensive account of communication. Although this system is devised for both teaching and non-teaching settings, it is particularly pertinent to language classrooms.

Different from FIAC and FLint, FOCUS shows the teacher's and the students' behaviours as interrelated. Moreover, it also takes into account non-verbal behaviours. This is important because, as Mehan points out, 'A description of the interconnected nature of teacher–student interaction in verbal and non-verbal modalities is required in order to capture the full range of activities that teachers and students engage in while coping with the complexities of classroom life' (1979:12).

One characteristic of FOCUS is that it aims to describe not only classrooms of all kinds by also non-classroom communication. For a system that aims to be as powerful as this, it is necessarily highly complex. The advantage of this is that the description is likely to be more comprehensive. The five dimensions provide important information that enables the observer to encode the context and the function of the utterances in a communication situation. For example, the question 'How much is a ticket to Chicago?' in a language classroom can be a simulation of real-life situations or it can be a question for grammar practice; they serve different purposes in language teaching. It is also easier for the reader to reconstruct the situation by reading the codings. The disadvantage is that it is impossible to do real-time coding. Even if the coding is done on transcriptions, it may be too complex for teachers who wish to examine their own lessons relatively quickly, without having to spend hours over the data coding. One possibility, as Fanselow himself suggested, is to use only part of the system. For example, instead of using all the subcategories, we can use the major categories to get a rough picture of the overall communication, and then only apply the fine subcategories to the part that we wish to focus on. For example, if we wish to focus on the areas of content that are communicated in a lesson, then only the subcategories of content and their further subcategories need to be used to analyse the data (Fanselow 1977: 30).

5.4 Devising classroom observation instruments

Observation systems are devised with different purposes, and different systems would be necessary for different classroom settings. For example, FIAC and FLint are devised for teacher-fronted classrooms and would be unsuitable for descriptions of group work. Even if the classroom settings are similar, it would be unwise, if not impossible, to adopt a system without any modifications since we may wish to focus on a particular aspect of interaction that the system does not specifically cater for. For example, if we wish to investigate the types of teacher question and their effect on student response, we will find that none of the systems examined above can serve that purpose. We need to set up many subcategories of questions in our system.

In the process of drawing up categories for the system, it is important to overcome the limitation of using predetermined categories and then forcing the data into the categories. This problem can be overcome if we start off with a very rough framework that we are prepared to modify or even discard, and if we modify existing categories or set up new categories when necessary. However, it is important to bear in mind that we should not indulge in the endless proliferation of categories, because this not only makes the system too complex even for ourselves to handle but makes it difficult for a reader to reconstruct the overall picture.

5.5 Ethnographic classroom observation

As pointed out in 5.2, one inherent limitation of systematic observation is that it does not provide evidence on the unobservables, such as participants' thinking behind their actions and their perceptions of other participants' actions. This is a serious limitation since these unobservables are often crucial in helping us understand the complexities of classroom processes. This is why more recent studies of classrooms have strongly advocated an alternative approach: ethnographic observation.

Instead of looking at a large number of classrooms, ethnographic observations often study in detail a single classroom or a single phenomenon in a small number of classrooms. Rather than looking for data that will fit into predetermined categories, ethnographic observations use an 'open-ended' approach, where the categories, if there are any, are derived from the data. The aim is to reconstruct the characteristics of the situation so that the reader can envision the same scene as witnessed by the researcher.

The following are some of the important characteristics of an ethnographic approach to observations. Firstly, it investigates an event or a situation from the participants' perception rather than from an outsider's interpretation of the event. Secondly, it is empirical and naturalistic. Both participant and non-participant observations are used to acquire first-hand accounts of the event in natural settings. Thirdly, the investigation is holistic. It tries to construct a description of the total event within its context in order to find out the complex interrelationships among the elements in the event. Fourthly, it is eclectic. A variety of data collection techniques is used so that data collected in one way can be cross-checked with data collected in another way (Goetz and Lecompte 1984). Erickson (1981) neatly summarizes the sources of data for ethnographic studies as 'asking' and 'watching'. 'Asking' refers to eliciting data from participants by using questionnaires and interviews; 'watching' refers to observation, both participant and non-participant. In addition to these two sources, documents and products are studied. For example, in classroom ethnographic studies, the documents would include lesson plans, school records, diaries, student work and so on. In the past twenty years, discourse analysis has become a very important component of data analysis in ethnographic studies (Watson-Gegeo 1988).

Despite the fact that there is a large number of ethnographic studies on classrooms, there are very few on language classrooms, and fewer on L2 classrooms. Most of the studies on language classrooms are either quantitative studies of the experimental kind or the application of a pre-specified model to the analysis of classroom data, with little or no attention to the nature of the classroom as a social context and with no evidence regarding the participants' perceptions of the events. Hence the two guiding principles of ethnographic studies are absent.

Since the seventies there has been a rapid growth of ethnographic studies. However, recent work has pointed out that while an ethnographic approach enables the researcher to discover new empirical facts and develop new theoretical ideas, it is inadequate in theory testing and development. Hammersley calls for researchers to treat systematic observation and ethnographic studies as complementary rather than as 'self-contained and mutually exclusive paradigms' (1986: 47). He points out that the process of decision making in classroom research is very complex and that we are more likely to find solutions to problems of classroom research if we maintain an 'open-ended attitude towards research, in which eclectic combinations of research methods can be used . . .' (Hammersley 1986: 47, citing Delamont and Hamilton 1984: 23–4).

SUMMARY

- Systematic observation makes explicit the aspects of classroom interaction under investigation and allows us to focus our attention on those aspects.

- The use of predetermined categories and coding the data without taking into consideration its full context are limitations of systematic observation, but these limitations can be overcome by deriving the categories from the data rather than forcing the latter into the former.
- An inherent limitation of descriptive systems of any kind is that, no matter how detailed the analysis, there is an important perspective missing from the data: the participants' perspective. This is where the ethnographic approach to classroom studies is superior.
- The two approaches to classroom observation – systematic observation and ethnographic study – should be used complementarily rather than exclusively.

Further Reading

Chapter 1

Allwright, D. and **K. Bailey.** 1991. *Focus on the Language Classroom*. New York: Cambridge University Press.

A detailed discussion of the important aspects of classroom interaction.

Wells, G. 1986. *The Meaning Makers*. London: Hodder and Stoughton.

A very good introduction to the relationship between language and learning. Wells uses plenty of data from first-language content classrooms to illustrate how the kind of interaction generated affects the kind of opportunities that are made available for learning. The comparison between language used at home and at school is illuminating.

Chapter 2

Allwright and **Bailey** (1991), as above.

Chapters 5 and 6 contain the most comprehensive coverage of studies done on error treatment and correction.

Barnes, D. 1969. Language in the secondary classroom. In D. Barnes, J. Britton and H. Rosen. *Language, the Learner and the School*. Harmondsworth: Penguin.

Contains an introduction to the distinction between 'open' and 'closed' questions, and 'genuine' versus 'pseudo' questions.

Brown, G. 1978. *Lecturing and Explaining*. London: Methuen.

Contains the most detailed discussion so far on explanation.

Brown, G. and **S. Armstrong.** 1984. Explaining and Explanations.

In E. C. Wragg (ed.) *Classroom Teaching Skills*. London: Routledge.

Contains the report of a study on the explanations by student-teachers of content subjects.

Brown, G. and **E. C. Wragg.** 1993. *Questioning*. London: Routledge.

Contains a very accessible discussion of questioning together with plenty of practical activities for analysing questions in content lessons, as well as many interesting activities on explanation in content lessons.

Chapter 3

Allwright and **Bailey** (1991), as above.

Chapter 7 discusses input and interaction in second-language classrooms. Turn-allocation and turn-taking are discussed in detail.

Chaudron, C. 1988. *Second Language Classrooms*. Cambridge: Cambridge University Press.

Chapter 5 contains a section on the questioning behaviour of teachers where it discusses in detail question types, modifications of questions and questioning patterns. It also gives a detailed report on the studies done on these aspects.

Long, M. 1983. Native speaker/non-native speaker conversation and the negotiation of comprehensible input. *Applied Linguistics*, 4, 126–41.

The phenomenon of modified interaction between NS and NNS speakers is applied to the negotiation of comprehensible input in ESL classrooms.

Chapter 4

Allwright and **Bailey** (1991), as above.

Chapter 10 contains a section on anxiety and language learning where the basic concept of anxiety and its relation to language learning are briefly discussed.

Dune E. and **N. Bennett.** 1990. *Talking and Learning in Groups*. London: Macmillan.

A very practical guidebook on conducting group work.

Horwitz, E. and **D. Young** (eds.) 1991. *Language Anxiety – from theory and research to classroom implications*. Englewood Cliffs, NJ: Prentice Hall.

This is a very good introduction to the constructs of foreign language learning anxiety. It contains a selection of articles discussing such anxiety from various perspectives and reports on studies done in this area.

Long, M. and **P. Porter.** 1985. Group work, interlanguage talk and second language acquisition. *TESOL Quarterly*, 19, 207–28.

A good introduction to small group talk. The article discusses the pedagogical value and the psycholinguistic rationale of group work. It also summarizes studies on small group talk, comparing NS–NNS interaction with NNS–NNS interaction, teacher-fronted classrooms with group work, and small group work using different task types.

Chapter 5

Allwright, D. 1988. *Observations in the Language Classroom*. London: Longman.

Contains a detailed discussion of language classroom observation and a comprehensive review of all the major instruments.

Allwright and Bailey (1991), as above.

Some of the major observation instruments are presented in the appendices.

Hammersley, M. 1986. *Controversies in Classroom Research*. Milton Keynes: Open University Press.

Part 1 of this book outlines the controversy over the interactional analysis approach versus the ethnographic approach.

Hammersley, M. 1990. *Classroom Ethnography*. Milton Keynes: Open University Press.

In the first part of the book Hammersley reports some ethnographic studies he has done. The second part is a detailed discussion of the methodological and theoretical issues in classroom ethnography.

Van Lier, L. 1988. *The Classroom and the Language Learner*. London: Longman.

This books advocates an ethnographic approach to classroom studies and outlines some of the strategies and procedures adopted in ethnographic studies. It also introduces other approaches to classroom research, such as diary studies and case studies.

Glossary

Note: This is a selective glossary, including only those items that are not specifically or succinctly defined in the main text.

communication apprehension   Fear and anxiety generated when communicating with other people in situations such as social conversations, interviews or meetings.

comprehensible input   Input that can be understood. In classroom interaction, input often refers to the language used by the teacher. However, language used by a pupil also serves as input for other pupils.

English as a Second Language   This term can be used to refer to the status of English in a society where it is not the mother tongue but is used as a medium of communication in education, business or government. It can also be used to refer to the role of English for minority groups in English-speaking countries where English is used for social, business, government and educational purposes but is not the mother tongue of these group members.

English as a Foreign Language   This term refers to the status of English in a society where it is only taught as a subject in the classroom, and is not used as a medium of communication in education, business or government.

embedded question   A question in which another question is inserted, for example *'Can you tell me where the train station is?'* There are two 'questions' within this question. One is 'Can you tell me something?' and the other is 'Where is the train station?' The latter is embedded in the former.

ethnographic approach   An ethnographic approach to classroom interaction is one in which the researcher examines classroom language and interaction in its entire context, with no preconceived ideas. The researcher describes naturally occurring events in the classroom from the perspective of the participants.

interlanguage   The kind of language produced by second- or foreign-language learners who are still learning the language.

modification device   A device that is used to avoid or repair breakdown in communication. Some examples of these devices are requests for repetition, requests for confirmation, requests for clarification, and so on.

referent   The actual object or state of affairs in the real world to which a linguistic expression refers. For example, the referent for the word *'building'* is the object 'building'.

target language   The language that a learner is trying to learn.

References

Allwright, D. 1980. Turns, topics and tasks: patterns of participation in language learning and teaching. In D. Larsen-Freeman (ed.) *Discourse Analysis in Second Language Research*. Rowley, Mass: Newbury House.

Allwright, D. and K. Bailey. 1991. *Focus on the Language Classroom*. New York: Cambridge University Press.

Barnes, D. 1969. Language in the secondary classroom. In D. Barnes, J. Britton and H. Rosen. *Language, the Learner and the School*. Harmondsworth: Penguin.

Barnes, D. 1976. *From Communication to Curriculum*. London: Penguin.

Brown, G. A. and S. Armstrong. 1984. Explaining and explanations. In E. C. Wragg (ed.) *Classroom Teaching Skills*. London: Routledge.

Cathcart, R. and J. Olsen. 1976. Teachers' and students' preferences for correction of classroom conversation errors. In J. Fanselow and R. Crymes (eds.) *On TESOL '76*. Washington, DC: TESOL.

Chaudron, C. 1982. Vocabulary elaboration in teachers' speech to L2 learners. *Studies in Second Language Acquisition*, 4, 170–80.

Chaudron, C. 1988. *Second Language Classrooms*. Cambridge: Cambridge University Press.

Delamont, S. and D. Hamilton. 1976. Classroom research: a cautionary tale? In M. Stubbs and S. Delamont (eds.) *Explorations in Classroom Observation*. Chichester: John Wiley.

Delamont, S. and D. Hamilton. 1984. Revisiting classroom research: a continuing cautionary tale. In M. Hammersley (ed.) *Controversies in Classroom Research*. Milton Keynes: Open University Press. Also appeared in S. Delamont (ed.) *Readings in Interaction in the Classroom*. London: Methuen.

Dillon, J. T. 1988. *Teaching and Questioning – a manual of practice*. London: Croom Helm.

Doughty, C. and T. Pica. 1986. Information gap tasks: do they facilitate second language acquisition? *TESOL Quarterly*, 20, 305–25.

Duff, P. 1986. Another look at interlanguage talk: taking task to task. In R. Day (ed.) *Talking to Learn*. Rowley, Mass.: Newbury House.

Dune E. and **N. Bennett.** 1990. *Talking and Learning in Groups*. London: Macmillan.

Erickson, F. 1981. Some approaches to inquiry in school-community ethnography. In H. T. Trueba, G. P. Guthrie and H. P. Au. (eds.) *Culture and the Bilingual Classroom – studies in classroom ethnography*. Rowley, Mass.: Newbury House.

Fanselow, J. 1977. Beyond Rashomon: conceptualizing and describing the teaching act. *TESOL Quarterly*, 11, 17–29.

Flanders, N. 1970. *Analyzing Teaching Behaviour*. Reading, Mass.: Addison-Wesley.

Fullilove, J. 1992. An analysis of small group talk. Unpublished manuscript. Dept. of Curriculum Studies, University of Hong Kong.

Gaies, S. 1980. Classroom-centered research: some consumer guidelines. Paper presented at the Second Annual TESOL Summer Meeting, Albuquerque, NM.

Goetz, J. and **M. Lecompte.** 1984. *Ethnography and Qualitative Design in Educational Research*. New York: Academic Press.

Halliday, M. A. K. 1976. Intonation and meaning. In G. Kress (ed.) *Halliday – system and function in language*. London: Oxford University Press.

Hammersley, M. 1986. Revisiting Hamilton and Delamont: a cautionary note on the relationship between 'systematic observation' and ethnography. In M. Hammersley (ed.) *Controversies in Classroom Research*. Milton Keynes: Open University Press.

Hammersley, M. 1990. *Classroom Ethnography*. Milton Keynes: Open University Press.

Horwitz, E., M. Horwitz and **J. Cope.** 1991. Foreign language classroom anxiety. In E. Horwitz and D. Young (eds.) *Language Anxiety – from theory and research to classroom implications*. Englewood Cliffs, NJ: Prentice Hall.

Kleinmann, H. 1977. Avoidance behaviour in adult second language learning. *Language Learning*, 27, 93–107.

Krashen, S. 1977. Some issues relating to the Monitor Model. In H. D. Brown, C. A. Yorio and R. H. Crymes (eds.) *On TESOL '77, Teaching and Learning English as a Second Language – trends in research and practice*. Washington, DC: TESOL.

References

Krashen, S. 1982. *Principles and Practice in Second Language Acquisition*. Oxford: Pergamon Press.

Krashen, S. 1983. Newmark's 'ignorance hypothesis' and current second language acquisition theory. In S. Gass and L. Selinker (eds.) *Language Transfer in Language Learning*. Rowley, Mass.: Newbury House.

Krashen, S. 1985. *The Input Hypothesis – issues and implications*. London: Longman.

Lee, A. 1993a. An analysis of comprehensible input and modified interaction in teacher-fronted talk and student group talk. Unpublished manuscript, Dept. of Curriculum Studies, University of Hong Kong.

Lee, A. 1993b. A study of vocabulary explanations in the intermediate EFL classroom: the variety and effectiveness of strategies employed. Unpublished M.Ed. dissertation, Dept. of Curriculum Studies, University of Hong Kong.

Long, M. 1975. Group work and communicative competence in the ESOL classroom. In M. K. Burt and H. C. Dulay (eds.) *On TESOL '75 – new directions in second language learning, teaching and bilingual education*. Washington, DC: TESOL.

Long, M. 1977. Teacher feedback on learner error: mapping cognitions. In H. D. Brown, C. A. Yorio and R. H. Crymes (eds.) *On TESOL '77, Teaching and Learning English as a Second Language – trends in research and practice*. Washington, DC: TESOL.

Long, M. 1983a. Does second language instruction make a difference? *TESOL Quarterly*, 17, 359–82.

Long, M. 1983b. Native speaker/non-native speaker conversation and the negotiation of comprehensible input. *Applied Linguistics*, 4, 126–41.

Long, M. and P. Porter. 1985. Group work, interlanguage talk and second language acquisition. *TESOL Quarterly*, 19, 207–28.

Long, M. and C. Sato 1983. Classroom foreigner talk discourse: forms and functions of teachers' questions. In H. W. Seliger and M. H. Long (eds.) *Classroom Oriented Research in Second Language Acquisition*. Rowley, Mass.: Newbury House.

McIntyre, D. and G. Macleod. 1986. The characteristics and uses of systematic observation. In M. Hammersley (ed.) *Controversies in Classroom Research*. Milton Keynes: Open University Press.

Martin, J. R. 1970. *Explaining, Understanding and Teaching*. New York McGraw-Hill.

Mehan, H. 1979. *Learning Lessons – social organization in the classroom.* Cambridge, Mass.: Harvard University Press.

Morgan, N. and **J. Saxton.** 1991. *Teaching, Questioning and Learning.* London: Routledge.

Moskowitz, G. 1967. The FLint system: an observational tool for the foreign language classroom. In A. Simon and E. G. Boyer (eds.) *Mirrors for Behavior – an anthology of classroom observation instruments.* Philadelphia, Pa.: Temple University.

Nation, P. 1990. *Teaching and Learning Vocabulary.* Rowley, Mass.: Newbury House.

Sato, C. 1982. Ethnic styles in classroom discourse. In M. Hines and W. Rutherford (eds.) *On TESOL '82.* Washington, DC: TESOL.

Scovel, T. 1978. The effect of affect on foreign language learning: a review of the anxiety research. *Language Learning,* 28, 129–42.

Seliger, H. W. 1983. Learner interaction in the classroom and its effect on language acquisition. In H. W. Seliger and M. Long (eds.) *Classroom oriented research in second language acquisition.* Rowley, Mass.: Newbury House.

Seliger, H. W. and **M. H. Long** (eds.) 1983. *Classroom Oriented Research in Second Language Acquisition.* Rowley, Mass.: Newbury House.

Sinclair, J. and **M. Coulthard** 1975. *Towards an Analysis of Discourse.* London: Oxford University Press.

Steinberg, F. and **E. Horwitz.** 1986. The effect of induced anxiety on the denotative and interpretive content of second language speech. *TESOL Quarterly,* 20, 131–6.

Swain, M. 1985. Communicative competence: some roles of comprehensible input and comprehensible output in its development. In S. Gass and C. Madden (eds.) *Input in Second Language Acquisition.* Rowley, Mass.: Newbury House.

ui, A. B. M. 1985. Analyzing input and interaction in second language lassrooms. *RELC Journal,* 16, 1, 8–32.

A. B. M. 1989. Beyond the adjacency pair. *Language in Society,* 18, 15–64.

B. M. 1992. Classroom discourse analysis in ESL teacher on. *ILE Journal,* 9, 81–96.

M. Forthcoming. Reticence and anxiety in second language n K. Bailey and D. Nunan (eds.) *Voices from the Classroom.* or publication.

References

Van Lier, L. 1988. *The Classroom and the Language Learner*. London: Longman.

Varonis, E. and S. Gass. 1985. Non-native/non-native conversations: a model for negotiation of meaning. *Applied Linguistics*, 6, 71–90.

Walker, Liz. Ongoing. The relationship between learner age and anxiety in foreign language learning, with special reference to oral communication in foreign language learning. Research project, Dept. of Curriculum Studies, University of Hong Kong.

Watson-Gegeo, K. A. 1988. Ethnography in ESL: defining the essentials. *TESOL Quarterly*, 22, 575–92.

Wells, G. 1986. *The Meaning Makers*. London: Hodder and Stoughton.

White, J. and P. Lightbown. 1984. Asking and answering in ESL classes. *Canadian Modern Language Review*, 40, 228–44.

Wood, D. J., L. McMahon and Y. Cranstourt. 1980. *Working with Under Fives*. Oxford: Basil Blackwell.

Wu, K. Y. 1991. Classroom interaction and teacher questions revisited. Unpublished manuscript. Dept. of Curriculum Studies, University of Hong Kong.

Wu, K. Y. 1993. Classroom interaction and teacher question revisited. *RELC Journal*, 24, 2, 49–68.

Index

Index